T5-CFQ-365

THEOLOGICAL THINKING
An In-quiry

American Academy of Religion
Studies in Religion

Editor
Lawrence S. Cunningham

ÆR

Number 53
THEOLOGICAL THINKING
An In-quiry
by
Carl Raschke

THEOLOGICAL THINKING
An In-quiry

by
Carl Raschke

Scholars Press
Atlanta, Georgia

BR
118
.R37
1988

THEOLOGICAL THINKING
An In-quiry

by
Carl Raschke

© 1988
The American Academy of Religion

Library of Congress Cataloging in Publication Data

Raschke, Carl A.
  Theological thinking.

  (Studies in religion / American Academy of Religion ;
no. 53)
  Includes bibliographical references.
  1. Theology—Methodology. I. Title. II. Series:
Studies in religion (American Academy of Religion) ;
no. 53.
  BR118.R37 1988   230'.01   87-26604
  ISBN 1-55540-187-2 (alk. paper)
  ISBN 1-55540-188-0 (pbk.: alk. paper)

Printed in the United States of America
on acid-free paper

TABLE OF CONTENTS

FOREWORD

To "think", as the Teutonic etymology of the term implies, is the same as to "thank", to respond with profound sincerity and gratitude. To "inquire", as the Latin root *quaero* discloses, is to "search inside", or "to question within", but not at all in a superficial manner. *Inquiry* means a searching and a questing/questioning that does not glide and ramble across the surface of things, but *dives into their very depths*. Questioning in this latter sense comes to be the utmost aim of all thought. Or, as the philosopher Martin Heidegger has put it so sententiously, "questioning is the piety of thinking". In a different manner of speaking, we may add: "thinking", which connotes much the same as "inquiry", is an *insearching*, not necessarily in the crypto-metaphysical context that "depth psychologists" have in mind when they invoke such a locution, but with a force similar to when we thoroughly explore what is present before us. Such a force is suggested in the word "inquest," which has an identical derivation. An inquest is a full and far-reaching examination of the background as well as the submerged indications of a claim or an event. It frequently refers to an investigation surrounding a mysterious death. It is our task here not to be concerned simply with thinking, but with *theological thinking*. The inquiry that amounts to thinking theologically may be regarded as a kind of "inquest" into the mysterious contention that "God is dead", for which the corollary is that theology has "ended".

Yet, as we shall discover, any proper inquest begins with a claim and concludes with a set of "revelations." The revelatory power of thought, which does not involve simply the "thinking of thoughts" but in Heidegger's phraseology a "thinking the unthought", is shown when thinking passes beyond itself, "deconstructs" itself, and enters into the tenebrous abyss of what has hitherto been censored from its domain. To think in this region of thought is to think theologically, which paradoxically embraces what theology in the past has never thought. Theology and theological thinking are, as Jacques Derrida, the great epigone of Heidegger might say, constituted by the great moment of *difference*. Theology is to theological thinking as everyday conversation is to psychoanalysis, as data is to theory, as description is to hypothesis. When theology ends, theological thinking commences in the most radical and provocative way of stating the matter. Theology is a discipline that has lost all but its most pedestrian disciples. Theological thinking is a return to the unthought origins of the discipline itself. Again, we must quote Heidegger: ". . . the essential nature of thinking, the essential origin of thinking, the essential possibilities of thinking—they are all strange to us, and by that very fact they are what gives us food for thought before else and always; which is not surprising if the assertion remains true that what is most thought-provoking in our thought-provoking age is that *we are still not thinking.*"* Theological thinking itself, therefore, wears the habit of the *viator,* the cloak of the stranger who confronts what is "strange" and not yet made accessible to thought. Theological thinking, in both a real and metaphorical sense, starts with the call of Abraham and ends up wandering amidst the nihilism of the present age. But strangely, what is called "theology" has both forgotten Abraham and has sought to codify its own nihilistic longings. It talks of "method" and means the fatality of self-reference. It endeavors in the madness of such "methodism" to *enclose the infinite.* It no longer remembers its origins, or foments an eschatology. Truly, that is part of what Nietzsche's madman contemplated when he proclaimed that God had died.

Theological thinking is eschatological thinking in the sense that it is preoccupied not just with alpha, but with omega. And in that regard it is thinking through and beyond what discloses itself through thought, a thinking which becomes a "faithful" kind of attention to the One in relationship to whom thinking is truly *thanking.* Yet the *fides* of "faithfulness", as Augustine realized, is also a *quaerans,* a questioning and a seeking in the direction of *intellectum,* an "understanding" or, more literally, a "reading between the lines". Faith also is inquiry. It is the depth of thinking.

Theological thinking, therefore, requires that the unthought must be recognized within the different domains and methods of thinking overall. Theological thinking does not count as a division of thought; it was never intended, even by Plato and the earliest Christian thinkers, as such. Theological thinking constitutes a relentless probing and rumination concerning what the Greeks, who are the earliest "theologians" on record, named *ho theos,* what is "holy" or "divine". As Heidegger has noted, the original Greek appreciation of "thinking" suffered amnesia at the hands of the "logicians", who transformed the primordial sense of *ho theos* into the "metaphysical" concept of *prote ousia,* the "Being" above beings. The heritage of Western theology, which is saturated with the metaphysical attitude, has been founded on this antique "category mistake".

Our task, therefore, is to recover the piety of thinking, which we denote as "theological thinking" in its originary mode. Because theological thinking endeavors to recover the unthought of the tradition of thought, to say what has remained "unsaid", to bring to light what has all along been closeted in the darkness where can also be found the unsculpted lineaments of time and discourse, its discursive range must entail much more than what con-

---

*Martin Heidegger, *What is Called Thinking,* trans. J. Glenn Gray (New York: Harper & Row, 1968), p. 45. Emphasis mine.

ventionally has been bounded as the province of "theology". Theological thinking *as thinking* shatters the very epistemic foundations of historical thought in its unfoldment. Theological thinking slips beneath the rudiments of epistemology and becomes ontology, or more exactly, a *heterology*, a meditation upon "otherness". Theological thinking is heterology. Whereas ontology, even in the sense of "fundamental ontology" articulated by Heidegger, calls us to the consideration of Being as it is revealed in language and culture, heterology draws us into the final "deconstructive" epiphany when even the ultimate name is eclipsed, when the most immense of idols, Derrida's "transcended signified", is effaced, and *faith* returns. Heterology, as well as faith itself, is founded upon the radical perplexity of present absence and absent presence, which even more strangely, like a sudden and world-circuiting lightning flash, reveals the Presence of the One who is ever present, having conquered time through the temporalizing of time itself. Theological thinking, therefore, means we must return to the kind of theological discernment once demanded by Karl Barth, albeit not the dogmatic Barth, but the Barth who in *The Epistle to the Romans* wrote: "The stone has been rolled away from the door of the tomb. The Word has free course."

Because theological thinking is a genuine thinking into the depths of thought, as well as a speaking of the unspoken of discourse, *as discourse* it must become "conversant" with the different grammars of difference. It has been the benchmark of late modern or, as some might call it, "post-modern" thinking to find the point of difference, the lapse in the putative foundation, in what were once regarded as impermeable battlements of reflection and argument. Henceforth, theological thinking must think through these paradigmatic modes of thought. The first mode of thinking is science, which achieves its moment of deconstruction in quantum physics. The second is hermeneutics, which passes over into the irreducible thought of the difference between how language is and the way in which language means. All hermeneutics eventually leads to a *deposing* of the theory of reference. And, finally, the realization that the end of the theory of reference debouches in what we shall call the "hermeneutics of the infinite" turns upon an appeal to the touchstone of scripture. By scripture we do not mean simply "sacred text." We mean a "texture" of significations for which the weave is unconditionally open. We mean, in the last analysis, the "deconstruction of the text of God". As our work discloses, the word "deconstruction," which has become a shibboleth for some and an affront for others, becomes, when appropriately heard in context, the key to the tradition of theology itself. The history of theology from beginning to end is the deconstruction of the word "God". The transition from theology to theological thinking is the resurrection of the *logos* in its own depths.

I should like to thank the University of Denver for modest sabbatical time to putter with the original draft of this book. I should also like to express gratitude to Prof. Charles Winquist of Syracuse University for his helpful reading of the manuscript. And, of course, I would like to voice my most loving appreciation to my wife, Susan, who since our first meeting has unfailingly encouraged me to "think the unthought".

Palmer Lake, Colorado
December, 1986

SECTION I

WHAT IS THEOLOGICAL THINKING?

CHAPTER I

THEOLOGICAL THINKING

"What is originality? To something that has no name as yet and
hence cannot be mentioned, although it stares us in the face."
—FRIEDRICH NIETZSCHE

Perhaps the greatest weakness in modern thought has been an inatten-
tion to the theological dimension of thinking. The neglect of theological
thinking has led not only to the demise of what was once the premier
"science," but to the slow deterioration of the various habits on intellectual
probing. Philosophy, once the unitary quest for wisdom, has devolved into
an overly cultivated subspecialty of linguistics and theoretical mathematics,
which neither challenges nor clarifies those forms of discrete inquiry. Without its theological leaven, historical research for the most part has lapsed into
a fruitless gathering and sorting of the givens of collective experience. And
what still goes by the name on "theology" nowadays is but a pallid imitation
of the numerous empirical fields of investigation.

When theology after Kant and Schleiermacher sought to become the
self-articulation of the contents of what we now term "religious experience",
it delivered its own writ of refusal.[1] For the turning of the theological mind
away from "God," setting aside the transcendent aim of its traditional mode
of reflection, brought about a long decline in vigor and relevance that I have
elsewhere dubbed "the end of theology".[2] That a once vibrant and confident

---

[1] A redrafting of Schleiermacher's theological agenda within the context of twentieth century
"religious studies" can be found in David Tracy's account of fundamental theology. For Tracy,
fundamental theology is that reflective enterprise which takes as its point of departure "the
explicitly metaphysical or transcendental moment" embedded within the phenomenology of
religion. Tracy writes that "fundamental theology is chiefly concerned with, in its phenomenological moment, with our common human experience and, in its transcendental or
metaphysical moment, with the abstract, general, universal and necessary features of that
common experience, the main emphasis in these normative analyses of religion will be upon
some 'religious dimension' to our ordinary experience." *The Analogical Imagination: Christian
Theology and the Culture of Pluralism* (New York: Crossroads, 1981), p. 160. A more subtle and
complex, but equally sophisticated undertaking of this sort can be attributed to Wolfhart
Pannenburg in his recent book *Anthropology in Theological Perspective* (Philadelphia: The
Westminster Press, 1985).

[2] See Carl Raschke, *The Alchemy of the Word: Language and the End of Theology* (Missoula,
MT: Scholars Press, 1979).

discipline should lose its object and become lost in the labrynth of self-reference is a strange historical anomaly. It would almost be as if all physicists at one moment decided to abandon the search for the fundamental laws of the universe and instead devoted their time to arguing over the utility of differential equations. Or the situation might be compared to Plato's cave dwellers who after having staggered out of the darkness and beheld the sun, realized that they much preferred the contemplation of shadows.

Why has theological thinking retreated from its honored task? And what must be done to replenish the fountainhead of theological insight? The decline of theological thinking has its beginnings in the period of Renaissance and Reformation. Indeed, we may discern during this era many intellectual trends and tendencies which are cognate with the intellectual situation today, and which have contributed all along to the erosion of the position of "theology" per se.

On the one hand, Renaissance humanism shifted the axis of European reflection from the contemplation of divine "otherness" indicated by Scriptural ambiguity and liturgical mystery to a celebration of humanity's unique propensities and talents. The Italian humanists, preoccupied as they were with rhetoric and philology to the exclusion of serious philosophical inquiry, nonetheless succeeded in reviving the spirit of classical paganism. The humanist picture of the human as *in media re*, as an incipient god who can be equally swayed by the promptings of his own beastly appetites, was not merely a sentimental engrafting of forgotten ancient ideas onto conventional Catholic piety. It was a distinct and monumental change in the reference frame of metaphysical thought. The humanist critique of Scholasticism, moreover, represented something quite more deep-reaching and complex than a disdain for turgid style and ecclesiastical pettifoggery. It showed that the traditional theological theme of citing God, whether as an ontological principle or as a redemptive agent, at the outset of all other adventures in discourse or "scientific" inquiries had suddenly been abridged. And it was this abridgement that truly gave rise to the mentality we know as the "modern."

On the other hand, the Protestant Reformation—which many historians have seen, especially in Calvin and Lutheran orthodoxy, as a reaffirmation of the Medieval attitude over against the relativizing tendencies of neoclassical scholarship and penitential morality—did not staunch the tide that was gradually washing away theology's position of sovereignty. A good case can be made, and has indeed been advanced over the years on various occasions, that Luther's strictly soteriological approach to fundamental theological issues set the course for the later dominance of German pietism and Romantic subjectivism.

It can also be said that Luther was primarily responsible for the anthropicization, and hence the total inversion, of the theological enterprise.

In declaring that theology is really anthropology, Feuerbach (good Hegelian that he was) merely made explicit what had already become a commonplace in Teutonic circles of learning. Yet the so-called "Protestant principle" itself was a major factor in the subtle swing toward reductionism that characterized the climate of opinion following the demise of orthodoxy. It was not so much the Enlightenment assault on dogmatism and "superstition" that drove theology ultimately into the arms of the historians, psychologists, and sociologists as it was the internal dialectic of Protestant ideology, which can be found in Calvinism as well as Lutheranism. Calvin's foundational dictum that "the finite cannot contain the infinite" (*finitum non capax infiniti*), which was shared by his Wittenberg colleague, had the effect of canceling out theology as a form of thinking and installing it as a mode of symbolic assent. By "symbolic assent" I mean the use of figurative or performative language to evoke a sense of reality and an objective presence for what otherwise cannot be communicated. It is both interesting and ironic that the transformation during the sixteenth century of metaphysical into metaphorical discourse within the domain of theology proper, as evidenced in the disputes over the nature of the sacraments, was matched by a movement within the sphere of hermeneutics or Scriptural interpretation from symbolism to literalism. This paradox has not been properly appreciated by historians of theology. But its long-range consequences are striking. It led to the dilution of whatever remained of Protestant theology's claims to being, or becoming, a "science" and to the reifying of evangelical forms of expression.

This trend toward reflection can be glimpsed in the familiar passage of Calvin's *Institutes* where the dialectic of divine knowledge and self-consciousness, known as the *duplex cognitio*, is set forth. "Nearly all the wisdom we possess, that is to say, true and sound wisdom, consists of two parts: the knowledge of God and of ourselves . . . no one can look upon himself without immediately turning his thoughts to the contemplation of God, in whom he 'lives and moves' . . . For, quite clearly, the mighty gifts with which we are endowed are hardly from ourselves; indeed, our very being is nothing but subsistence in the one God. Then, by these benefits shed like dew from heaven upon us, we are led as by rivulets to the spring itself. Indeed, our very poverty better discloses the infinitude of benefits reposing in God."[3]

Calvin concludes: "it is certain that man never achieve a clear knowledge of himself unless he has first looked upon God's face and then descends from contemplating him to scrutinize himself."[4] Scholars intimate with Calvin's work are aware that the Genevan theologian relaxed the tension of the *duplex cognitio* by asserting the absolute authority and salvific power of Scriptural

[3] John Calvin, *Selections*, ed. by John Dillenberger (Missoula, MT: Scholars Press, 1975), p. 320.

[4] Calvin, p. 321.

reading. Inasmuch as the perception of an unqualifiable and inscrutable Deity is set over against the "misery" and sense of abasement arising from the experience of selfhood, there can, for Calvin, be no positive knowledge generated by either "theology" in its classic stance or psychology in its general form. The "double knowledge" of God and self constitutes an aporia, a seemingly irresolvable contradiction. The entire cognitive relationship is what in the modern context we would term "existential." Thus theology becomes soteriology, converting all possible "thinking" about God into the purely subjective position of "faith". And faith itself is supported according to Calvin, by "the word of God" as its "object and target."[5]

The holy word, however, is not a datum for understanding; it is an occasion for response. Protestant hermeneutics, culminating in Bultmann, came to rest upon a distinct lack of attention to the noetic content of Scripture in combination with an overemphasis on personal disposition and behavior. The "anthropological" bias of Protestant theology emerged in the very beginning. And because the "word" as stimulus and summons was made the central focus of Protestant inquiry into God's character and purpose, the idiom of Biblical revelation—what Aquinas had called "sacred doctrine"— paradoxically became useless to the religious thinker except as a stock incentive for pious confession and moral action. No longer could it be construed as having any bearing upon the broader order of knowledge. Only what Protestant divines regarded as "special revelation" counted any longer. And the analysis of special revelation was really a task for Christian ethics and historiography.

The philosophical codification of this peculiar outlook was accomplished with Kant's division of "practical" from "theoretical" reason. Theological matters, for Kant, are dissolved into the heuristic representation of moral aims and projects. As Kant put the matter in his *Religion within the Limits of Reason Alone*, the "idea" of God "arises out of morality and is not its basis; it is an end the adoption of which as one's own presupposes basic ethical principles."[6] Kant's translation of the complete set of theological issues into a relatively unspecified program of a "moral anthropology" inspiring most of the nineteenth century's agenda, was directly accountable for the eclipse of theological thinking. The older Protestant preoccupation with the personal aims of "justification" and "sanctification" was now enshrined in a unique kind of metaphysical solipsism which, on the one hand, sanctioned without reservations the new empirical sciences and, on the other hand, served to bracket all autonomous theological questions concerning what Kant himself referred to as "transcendent" subject matter. The *duplex cognitio* was rein- vented as Kant's metaphysical "antinomies"—what he called "the conflict

[5]Calvin, p. 274.

[6]Immanuel Kant, *Religion within the Limits of Reason Alone*, trans. Theodore M. Greene and Hoyt H. Hudson (New York: Harper & Row, 1960), p. 7.

between different kinds of apparently dogmatical knowledge"[7]—the discovery of which in turn cast suspicion upon all religiously definitive, or "speculative", truths.

It was Kant's devastating critique of the "pretensions" of metaphysics, which apart from Christian devotional literature had been the staple for theological reasoning, that caused the methodological retreat to the subject during the nineteenth century. Theological thinking, at least since Augustine, has always been distinguished by its audacious reach beyond the limits of conventional understanding. That drive of the theological intellect is empowered by the movement of faith.

Theological thinking has always been established on what in Kantian phraseology we might describe as the "interest" of faith—a faith that inclines the mind to take wing and yearn to attain the stars. It is reason, however, that steers the flight and sets its destination. The intimate correlation between faith and reason was the regulative principle for theological inquiry up until the Reformation. The Reformation squabbles over the grounds of religious and theological authority, which ultimately divided into the supremacy of the Biblical text on the Protestant side and conciliar autarky in the Catholic camp, laid waste to this sense of the correlation. The segregation of theological thinking into an unreflective scholasticism and an introverted pietism, which had been the trend anyway since the fourteenth century, gave rise to a double-mindedness, and an anxiety over the basis upon which the discipline might certified, that slowly and tediously for half a millenium drained its energy.

At the death of Kant theological thinking, once the "queen" of the sciences, was now about to descend into an occult occupation. The transformation of theological thinking into occultism can be chiefly accredited to Schleiermacher.

It was Schleiermacher who resolutely set aside "doctrine" (Glaubenslehre) as the foundation for "theological reflection" and installed what he alternately termed "feeling", "piety," and "religious self-consciousness." Religious self-consciousness, as Schleiermacher made clear both in his Speeches and in his later treatise on dogmatics known as The Christian Faith, is an inherent virtue of the human species. It is what we ordinarily mean by "faith," which takes no supernatural object, but connotes an indwelling gift or genius that is closely related to aesthetic sensibility. The Christian stance is simply one of sharing in the consummate religious self-knowledge, or "God consciousness" of the historical figure we recall as the Redeemer. Jesus himself was a supremely evolved religious personality. "There is no reason why we should not believe," Schleiermacher wrote in The Christian Faith, that the appearing of such a life is the result of the

---

[7] Immanuel Kant, Critique of Pure Reason, trans. F. Max Mueller (Garden City, NY: Doubleday, 1966), p. 303.

power of development which resides in our human nature—a power which expresses itself in particular men at particular points according to laws which, if hidden from us, are nevertheless of divine arrangement, in order through these men to help the others forward."[8]

The idea of redemption as apotheosis, as the evolution of an unsurpassed spiritual awareness, was of course an ancient Gnostic motif that passed through the Hermetic revival of the sixteenth century into the culture of Romanticism, where it subsequently became codified as the theosophical illuminism that grew fashionable around 1890.[9] Theosophical illuminism, or what might better be characterized as "esoteric psychology," was the natural heir to Kant's moral subjectivity. For, like Kant's revisionist "eschatology" laid out in *The Critique of Practical Reason*, it viewed God as a construct of human striving. It made theology an extension of what the Germans regarded as *Bildung*, or "self-formation," the state of "inwardness" which the Romantics so astutely prized. The "occultist" tendencies in post-Kantian religious thought can be glimpsed in its swerve away from traditional, confessional language and its emphasis on the idiosyncrasies of religious experience, what Schleiermacher cryptically described as "the supernatural becoming natural."

But nineteenth century theological naturalism was far different from the varieties of metaphysical naturalism that made up the ideological grist for both Anglican and Continental philosophy. Theological naturalism was actually an upside-down dogmatics, stressing the Protean dimensions of experience as a foil for propositional truth, the heretical over the clerical, what would later be christened the "unconscious" in preference to rational belief. The cultivation of a "natural supernaturalism," which is one famous literary critic's designation for the whole of the Romantic theory of interpretation,[10] brought with it a strange convolution of the historically endowed theological task. Nietzsche's acid critique of Christian morality, combined with his glorification of the will in a poetic attempt to "deconstruct" the concept of divine agency, could only have come about as a consequence of the process of inversion. Nietzsche sought to recapture "original" thinking through semantic dances, arch allusions to the primordial, and sustained attacks on "the moral interpretation" of the world. His seeming hostility to theological thinking, however, was but a rhetorical feint in light of the movement of

---

[8] Friedrich Schleiermacher, *The Christian Faith*, trans. H. R. Mackintosh and J. W. Stewart (Edinburgh: T. & T. Clark, 1968), p. 63.

[9] For an historical overview of these developments, see my own book, *The Interruption of Eternity: Modern Gnosticism and the Origins of the New Religious Consciousness* (Chicago: Nelson-Hall, 1980).

[10] See M. H. Abrams, *Natural Supernaturalism* (New York: W. W. Norton, 1971. Abrams sees in Romanticism as a movement "the secularization of inherited theological ideas and ways of thinking" (p. 12), hence the title.

theology itself in the direction Nietzsche would have lauded as "anti-Christian" and heroically pagan.

Theology in the nineteenth century lost its object, and was gradually converted into a hermeneutics of self-reflection, culminating in the atheistic existentialism of Tillich and the heuristic Christianity of Bultmann. The drift of theology away from its dogmatic foundations and into the twilight land of existential psychology was more consequential than could have been foreseen even until recently. For this transposition had the effect of abrogating once and for all the classic role of theology as a venture into matters transcendental, what Aquinas called "things under the formality of being divinely revealed."[11] It was not that theology eventually became confused about its "method," as some contemporary writers have maintained.[12] For the preoccupation with method could only have arisen when the aim had slipped from view. Theological thinking had become dispossessed of its own distinctive "formality," a basic ontological understanding that would have given some semantic ballast to the very word "God". The search for that formality is the quest for the restoration of theological thinking in an era when serious thinking of that order has been deemed well-nigh frivolous or impossible. We shall find, however, that theological thinking should not be abandoned, even at a time when "theology" per se as an ecclesiastical discipline has reached its point of closure.

[11] Thomas Aquinas, *Summa Theologica*, Q. 1, Art. 4.

[12] One of the foremost contemporary theological writers concerned about method is Gordon Kaufman. See his book *An Essay on Theological Method* (Missoula, MT: Scholars Press, 1975).

CHAPTER 2

HERMENEUTICS, SCIENCE, SCRIPTURE: THREE TRAJECTORIES TOWARD THE REHABILITATION OF THEOLOGICAL DISCOURSE

"Human experience and human perception end where God begins."

—KARL BARTH

In the altercation during the last ten years concerning theological "method," not to mention discussions about how to "ground" as well as bring to an "end" the conventions of God-language, a signal point has perhaps been slighted. That point is simply whether theological discourse can ever retain the vigor and semantic force of its own classic logos, whether the diction itself is still capable of self-transcendence, whether the grammar of divinity maintains any kind of paradoxical tension between the cultural conceits of "religious thinkers" and the splendor of the transcendent—what Kierkegaard appropriately dubbed "the incommensurable occasion."

The issue may be framed with even greater rigor: can theological thinking return from its recent exile in the vast negation of contemporary "experience"? The past two decades have witnessed the demise of what we have customarily known as theology and the regency of something diffuse, and often exotic, dubbed "religion." Theology has, in fact, been conveniently subsumed, probably far more for political than for indigenous reasons, under the academic scrutiny of general "religious" phenomena. Those who doggedly cleave to the title of "theologians" have nonetheless tended to spin their statements from broad religious assumptions. For example, outside evangelical circles and the undisturbed ramparts of orthodoxy, it is now a bland presupposition that any serious theological deduction must have been preceded by some careful assessment of the pluralistic features of the world's "traditions" as well as the personal varieties of "religious experience." This demand constitutes what we might describe as an *epistemological impact statement;* and like all similar impositions it has proven to be costly, time-consuming, and of dubious value nevertheless in helping preserve endangered species.

Yet such a disclaimer from the standpoint of theology is more than a compensatory, or even an exegetical, exercise. It amounts to a dismembering of the theological organism *tout d'un coup*. The warning of the early Barth concerning any sort of ontology with religion (which he defined as "that human necessity in which the power exercised over men by sin is clearly demonstrated") as its fulcrum clearly has lost its sting.[1] For it is not simply a problem that "sin" has been removed from our theological slate of interests. It also has to do with the fact that we no longer have a lodestar other than religion by which to pilot our deliberations.

At the same time, a theology erected on the scaffolding of religion must by its own internal logic be thoroughly "godless." For living gods do not normally admit of multivalent accounting; they require singular attention and veneration, if not a profound ascesis of the scholarly intellect. That is why historical polytheism—whether Greek, Indian, or Far Eastern—was overseen by priests and caretakers of shrines, not by theologians. Furthermore, the "God" of theology must somehow be exempt from any policy of reduction. It is the destiny of theology to have immolated itself in the quest for confirmation—and perhaps to rise anew ironically once the discovery has been made that the newly established rules for justification are sublimely irrelevant to the theological prospect.

But this promise is gainsaid when we survey how it has become the contemporary passion of theology to flagellate both its mission and its identity. The habit of flagellation traces back to the "radical theology" movement of the 1960s and the long-persisting quandry of liberal religious thinkers over how to talk sensibly about their subject matter.[2] When God "appeared" to them limp on the bier, the theological magisterium adopted the manner of bereaved next of kin, who instead of facing up to the death of the patriarch can only hold forth with polite trifles. Radical theology itself, like the political radicalism of that period, was but a short-lived experiment in liminality, a jerky transfer from ecclesial confession to what has become *prima face* a neo-pagan cosmopolitan sensibility swaddled with such convoluted monikers as "post-Christian pluralistic religiosity." The scourge of all methodological feints and stabs during this twilight era has been a point of

[1] Karl Barth, *The Epistle to the Romans*, trans. Edwyn C. Hoskyns (New York: Oxford University Press, 1968), p. 253.

[2] The "radical theology" movement, of course, is anchored in the metaphysics of *kenosis*, or God's "self-emptying," mentioned in Paul and structured into a cosmo-historical root metaphor by Thomas J. J. Altizer. See *inter alia* Thomas J. J. Altizer, *The Gospel of Christian Atheism* (Philadelphia: The Westminster Press, 1966); *The Self-Embodiment of God* (New York: Harper & Row, 1977). The *kenosis* is also, according to Altizer, an evacuation of the plenitude of the divine logos into silence. Thus, it has become historically inevitable that "theology today is in quest of a language and mode whereby it can speak of God . . . a quest for language itself . . . a language whereby we can actually and fully speak." *The Self-Embodiment of God*, p. 1.

view with a discrete sociology in the background. The point of view is braided from our secular "myth" associated oddly with the Bultmannian crusade for "de-mythologization." As a myth it has operated with its own lexemes—terms such as "human existence," "secular experience," "worldliness," etc. From a less complimentary stance we might construe the cognitive and ethical dimensions of this view as a unique sort of brew. We might denote it as *terminal Protestant nihilism*.

Indeed, the nihilistic texture of theological thinking since the 1960s has been openly avowed by David Tracy, who in *The Analogical Imagination* has written: "To pass through the sacred void of our own moment disallows any easy, clever, 'canny' refusal of the route of the *nihil* in our uncanny nihilism." And he adds, unwittingly paraphrasing the arch allusions of Nietzsche's madman in the marketplace: "For there is today in every text, every image, every act of interpretation, indeed every act, no origin, no center, no end, no correct, no right, not even a determinate meaning. There is, rather, the incessant play of signs in the labrynth, the web, the whirlpool . . ."[3] Tracy also gives us his sociological rationale in the first chapter. The rationale is the investiture of theology within the academy which, in this curious nuptials of Athens with Jerusalem, brings about a forced retirement of what has long been understood as the theological occupation. We quote once more Tracy: ". . . the realities of society and academy, the realities of our common human experience and disciplined reflection upon it cannot but enter our theological reflections on strictly theological grounds."[4] For Tracy, the hub of major theological meditations is a kind of social self-consciousness which is also ethnographic ("secular/professional) as well as academic. Tracy describes these meditations as "fundamental theology." Fundamental theology is essentially a transcendental analysis of secularity where God sneaks in as one symbological datum among others. Such a God is not the *Deus revelatus atque absconditus* of a two-thousand year tradition.

The masking of secular advocacy as "theological" discourse bespeaks, if we are to remain honest with ourselves, a quiet kind of suicide. But can we genuinely conceive of repairing theological conversation so that it will be neither (i) literary preciosity camouflaged as *demonstratio Christiana* (ii) the sort of pale Gnosticism or cultured hermeticism which we find now abundantly in Jungian psychology, "cross-cultural" religious philosophy, and the eclectic appeals to "myth" and "imagination" as wellsprings of our contrived post-Christian piety. Are we forever following Tracy's metaphor, wandering in the labrynth? The "fall" two decades ago may be ascribed, purely and straightforwardly, to an entrenched despair among Christian thinkers about

---

[3] David Tracy, *The Analogical Imagination: Christian Theology and the Culture of Pluralism* (New York: Crossroad, 1981), p. 360.
[4] Tracy, p. 49.

the neo-orthodox prohibition against all content assessements of the religious, linguistic, or "empirical" factors in theological inquiry. The loss of the *revelatum* created a diaspora.

Yet by now the diaspora has been so internalized that theological purpose itself has all but disappeared. "God-talk" has become virtually indistinguishable from omnibus chic-speak, illuministic mutterings, or outright psychobabble. The false dichotomy, barring us from a new theological ingathering, is between a muddy religious historicism and the old-style Barthian dialectics of *Krisis*.

Are there trajectories leading us immediately out of our pitiable, present day "religious situation"? The situation itself has become an Oz-like sojourn through the munificent metaphysical imagination of the modern. Ever since the meteoric display of radical theology expired, theologians (so-named) have been hankering after some wispy surrogate for the "Kingdom" under the innocuous caption of "transcendence" or the "transcendental".[5] The prospectus of post-radical transcendentalism happily coincided with the popular prepossession in the late Sixties and the decade of the 1970s with intra-conscious odysseys, mystical or "Dionysian" forays, and the socio-cultural fascination with the "Self", all under the expansive rubric of novel, unique, but ill-specified psycho-spirituality. Theologians sought to sink moorings in this sea of Protean longings. Tracy in his earlier book called for the establishment of his "fundamental theology" by anchoring its inductive procedures in the phenomenology of self-reflective, global "religious" experience. The canons of such a fundamental theology would rest on the principle of "meaning-as-internal-coherence", and the theological agenda per se would consist in the posing of "the explicit cognitive questions of the conditions for the possibility of the primordial experience of the self."[6] The "self" therefore in Tracy's urbane analysis serves as the Archimedean point for transcendental reflection. The viewpoint is decidedly neo-Romantic. Fichte or Schelling would have quibbles with the passage of theological thinking into metapsychology, which has taken place subtly but ineluctably in the last decade. And it is worth observing that discourse on the self has now secured its own *ordo significationis* in the application of Jungian theories and constructs to the theological idiom.[7]

---

[5]The literature of "transcendence" from the late 1960s and early 1970s is extensive. As examples: Herbert Richardson, *Transcendence* (Boston: Beacon Press, 1967); Alistair Kee, *The Way of Transcendence: Christian Faith Without Belief in God* (New York: Penguin Books, 1971; William A. Johnson, *The Search for Transcendence* (New York: Harper & Row, 1974).

[6]David Tracy, *Blessed Rage for Order: The New Pluralism in Theology* (New York: Seabury,1 975), p. 71.

[7]See, for example, Wallace Clift, *Jung and Christianity: The Challenge of Reconciliation* (New York: Crossroads, 1982). Clift does not seek to reduce Christian concepts and symbols to the Jungian language, but he sees a close interrelation between the two.

There are three possible trajectories we may elect to follow. Failure to pursue these paths may mean that we wind up deluged by the inclement tide of archaism. Instead of idly settling into a new kind of cosmo-sacral polytheism cousin to the outlook of the decadent Roman *imperium,* we must in the domain of "theology" find our center of gravity once more. Otherwise, the Krisis will surely and quite soon befall us.

The three trajectories, then, can be drawn from the dominant methodological formalities which have occupied theologians in the past. Theology has always been a mode of serious inquiry, not an apology for the modern mysteries. Such trajectories out of the dream state of "religion" can be enumerated as follows: (i) hermeneutics (ii) science (iii) Scripture.

*   *   *

"All theology," declared Barth, "is *theologia viatorum.*" Theology "does not exhibit its object but can only indicate it, and in doing so it owes the truth to the self-witness of the these and not to its own resources."[9] The *viator* or wayfarer, of course, is the archetype of faithfulness, whether the theme be instantiated in the figure of Abraham, the children of Israel, Christ as the "high priest" in the Epistle to the Hebrews, or Kierkegaard's knight *incognito.* Yet the *viator* stands too for the sojourner midway between alpha and omega, which are God's points of reference. He is not simply *in media re,* as the "theology on worldliness" maintains. The wayfarer finds himself in a state of liminality, which is to say that both the starting and resting points of his wanderings are neither evident nor perspicuous.[10]

Theology as the self-avowal of the pilgrim in Barth's sense can never be "grounded" in the strict, epistemological connotation of the term. That is why the fashion of deploying "ordinary language philosophy" for the sake of theological conundra has proven vapid and useless. Ordinary language philosophy is, and has always been, the "therapeutic" (Wittgenstein) reassembly of belief systems through conformance of their semantics with conventional norms of discourse. The grounding of theological contentions via the method of logical justification, or by the kind of appeal to propositional first principles known as "foundationalism," in the final summation turns out to be an elaborate form of question begging. For the foundationalist seeks to dispense with the problems of theological thinking by highlighting certain kinds of "basic beliefs" which seem to be rational only because they are necessary

---

[8] See my own article, "The Future of Religious Studies: Moving Beyond the Mandate of the 1960s," *Bulletin of the Council for the Study of Religion* 14 (1983): 146–8.

[9] Karl Barth, *Church Dogmatics,* trans. G. W. Bromiley (Edinburgh: T. & T. Clark, 1961), III, 3, 293.

[10] See Charles Winquist, "The Epistemology of Darkness: Preliminary Reflections," *Journal of the American Academy of Religion* 49 (1981): 24–43.

primitive components of a larger architecture of plausible views and tenets.[11] Such basic beliefs, nonetheless, are little more than generic codings for the kinds of obligatory religious professions which the devotee routinely makes and which are of little interest to the enterprise of theology specifically. In its more recent ventures foundationalism has proven to be but a dextrous reworking of old-style dogmatics, brandishing anew the stance of "theism" without ever addressing the profound epistemological questions that challenged "belief" in the first place.

It was this sort of substitution of a formalistic calculus for earnest intellectual inquiry which spurred Wittgenstein to make his historical remark that "the nimbus of philosophy has been lost."[2] The same can be said nowadays of the theological business. However, theology without a nimbus is like astronomy without the starry firmament. That is why hermeneutics comprises the indispensible first gesture in the rehabilitation of theological discourse. Hermeneutics serves to recommission the theological odyssey, to liberate it from the vapid stance of apologetics and to imbue it with a sense of adventure. The viator is always looking out for the promised land beyond the horizon.

A hermeneutical concern must be ingredient in all theological efforts because without it all talk about God must become a ravel of self-referring syntax. It has been Heidegger, of course, who has steered us toward an appreciation of the semic "infinity" of all linguistic acts and thereby stood sentinel against the tendency for philosophical and theological conversation to hurl itself into a carnival of the commonplace. Heidegger has reminded us that both philosophical and theological discourse remain lively by virtue of the hermeneutical task. Every batch of familiar issues is engrafted within an ensemble of communicative habits, and these habits must be constantly scrutinized by disclosing their history. It is their concealed etiology (to employ Freud's parlance, their "latency") which prevents any contemporary interpretation from collapsing into a catechism. For hermeneutics amounts essentially to the self-limiting activity of language as it coils back upon itself. Or, as Gadamer says, the hermeneutical moment is the event wherein the "self-forgetfulness that belongs to language" in its natural or naive estate is

---

[11] Some of the most important work on the subject of "foundational" knowledge from the philosophical standpoint is Roderick M. Chisholm, *The Foundations of Knowing* (Minneapolis, MN: The University of Minnesota Press, 1982); Keith Lehrer, *Knowledge* (Oxford: Clarendon Press, 1974); Noah Lemos, "Coherence and Epistemic Priority," *Philosophical Studies* 41 (1982): 299–315; Bruce Aune, "Epistemic Justification", *Philosophical Studies* 40 (1981): 419–29; Alan Goldman, "Epistemic Foundationalism and the Replaceability of Observation Language," *Journal of Philosophy* 22 (1982): 13–54. For recent discussions as they apply to theological claims and discussions about God, see Alvin Plantinga and Nicholas Wolterstorff (eds.), *Faith and Rationality: Reason and Belief in God* (Notre Dame: University of Notre Dame Press, 1983).

[12] Desmond Lee (ed.), *Wittgenstein's Lectures: Cambridge, 1930–1932* (Totowa, NJ: Rowman and Littlefield, 1980), p. 20.

dispelled. "To this extent," notes Gadamer, "language is the real mark of our finitude."[13] And we might add, therefore: hermeneutics as a mode of finite reflection is inescapably post-lapsarian, a token of fallenness.

At the same time, the "fallenness" which epitomizes the hermeneutical perspective does not mean theology is incapable of any meaningful assent. The hermeneutics of the early Heidegger, and likewise the "hermeneutical" obsession of the Bultmannian circle of twentieth century religious thinkers, always homed in upon the "existential" structures of human self-awareness. Theology persisted as a low-grade type of cultural anthropology. The "text" of theology was but the diary of modernity. Hermeneutics functioned as a form of self-exposition—we might even go so far as to call it a methodological narcissism, which had little to do with the standard theological agenda of explicating the data of divinity.

Still, it was Gadamer who first pointed to the way out of this subtle solipsism. Gadamer's *tour de force* was to refurbish the spirit of Romantic hermeneutics without centering on the "intention" of the author. For hermeneutics, according to Gadamer, draws its charge from the connotative richness—let us even say the "disclosive power"—of language itself. Hence hermeneutics begins and ends with the movement whereby language discovers both its own liminality and the extra-linguistic store of semantic potentialities. That is why Gadamer concludes his magnum opus on hermeneutics with the assertion: "language is not its elaborate conventionalism, nor the burden of pre-schematisation with which it loads us, but the generative and creative power unceasingly to make this whole fluid."[14] The hermeneutical penetration of the linguistic inscription performs a de facto theological role, insofar as it calls attention to the "nimbus" of our perennial speech. And it unchains theological discourse from the freckless protocols of propositional analysis. Thus the hermeneutical move means fundamentally that theology acquires once again an interest in the measures of "reference" rather than of merely "sense." The same motif is underscored by Paul Ricoeur, building on Gadamer. All hermeneutical understanding is an "appropriation" of the "revelatory power of the text".

Furthermore, "the link between appropriation and revelation is . . . the cornerstone of a hermeneutics which seeks both to overcome the failure of historicism and to remain faithful to the original intention of Romantic hermeneutics."[15] Hermeneutics in the primal version commended by Heidegger, Gadamer, and Ricoeur can never suffice for theological thinking in its classical cast. The polysemy of any given human utterance is never

[13] Hans-George Gadamer, *Philosophical Hermeneutics*, trans. David E. Linge (Berkeley, CA: University of California Press, 1976), p. 64.

[14] Hans-Georg Gadamer, *Truth and Method* (New York: Crossroad, 1982), p. 498.

[15] Paul Ricoeur, *Hermeneutics and the Human Sciences*, ed. and trans. John B. Thompson (London: Cambridge University Press, 1981), p. 191.

precisely equivalent to holy writ. Hermeneutics delves into dimensions of
experience where ordinary language rarely steps. But the shadows of the
finite should never be mistaken for the infinite refulgence. In this connection
the work of hermeneutics is chiefly to foster the "deconstruction" of all
exoteric traditions. Hermeneutics shows us that if theology is not to perish
from what Wallace Stevens once called "the stupor of banality," it must
always remain somewhat tenebrous in style as well as subject matter. If, for
example, the "salvation" doctrines of the New Testament had been as easy to
decipher as post-Reformation Protestant orthodoxy once averred, then the
Christian faith would never have been the "scandal" it remained from the
outset.

The call for hermeneutical inquiry into the semiotic makeup of any
sacred text arises from the fact that the writing itself, together with the
doctrinal and creedal baggage that has developed through time alongside it,
has enigmatic edges—i.e., a "nimbus". Thus the inaugural phase of a renewed theological commitment must comprise what Charles Winquist has
termed an "epistemology of darkness", a glance into the psychologically
dispossessed. Only when theology surveys the archives of its own long
evolving diction can it discover what is relatively substantial and what is a
mere contemporaneous contingency. It makes this distinction by assessing
what Gadamer dubs the "polarity of familiarity and strangeness on which
heremeneutic work is based."[17] Consciousness of such a polarity, which
belongs properly to any sense of a *traditio*, is what has heightened, if not
driven, theological work for over a millenia. Similarly, it is the erasure of
such a consciousness in the so-named "post-modern" decades that has raided
the vitality of theological labors as a whole.

Yet theological interest in what has been historically repressed, un-
detected, or must never become a methodological fascination. Such a fascination has already beset many of our new theologians who wish to work
from the standpoint of *religion* or "religious studies" as a nominal discipline. The Barthian condemnation of religion as "godless" is not to be taken
lightly by those with serious theological aims; for while the history and
anthropology of the mercurial phenomenon known as *religio* contains epi-
sodes of heroic transcendence and grandeur, it is also littered with supersti-
tions, fixations, and absurdities. At the very least "religious consciousness"—
as it has often been labelled since the nineteenth century—can never in itself
pass muster as a pure display for theological consideration. Whereas theological claims can always be shown in retrospect to have been limited by
religious or ideological factors, the two are not automatically commensurate
with each other.

---

[16] See Charles Winquist, "Theology, Deconstruction, and Ritual Process," *Zygon: Journal of
Religion and Science* 18 (1985): 295–310.
[17] *Truth and Method*, p. 262.

By the same token, the critique of theology from the angle of religious history, as well as from any specialized "hermeneutical" starting point, can never replace altogether the theological objective. It has been the sad plight of theological thinking since the Enlightenment to have defaulted so far from any recognizable avowal of its own legitimacy, that the current fashion now is to defend its cogency solely as a kind of belletristic artifice. We hear theology spoken of as "imaginative," "fictive," "metaphorical," etc.[18] The self-abnegation of a purely subjective theology is juxtaposed to the alleged sovereignty of "objective" science and its secular embodiments.

Yet it has been the element of *scientia* (the root meaning of the Latin term is "to decide" or "to determine") within the theological tradition that has kept it viable from one generation to the next. In classical and Medieval times, for instance, it was this "scientific" emphasis within theology that allowed genuine faith to be distinguished from pagan "myth" and *superstitio*. Only with German pietism, which has exerted a greater influence on the twentieth century liberal Protestant mind than we are willing to admit, did religious sensibility devoid of science acquire any notable authority. Thus the hermeneutical preoccupation of contemporary religious thought, which has won but a Pyhrric victory over orthodoxy, must yield once again to the "scientific" impulse inherent in all intellectual inquiry. Such a transition is now possible because of a new portrait of science itself.

The new understanding of science is summarized by philosopher Stephen Toulmin:

"We need . . . to see scientific thought and practice as a developing body of ideas and techniques. These ideas and methods, and even the controlling aims of science itself, are continually evolving, in a changing intellectual and social environment."[19]

Whereas theologians in recent years have tended to grant an unwarranted and undeserved epistemological privilege to modern science, both the practice and philosophy of science have sidled toward a relativization of their domain of investigation. Science as a pragmatic vehicle for "mapping" the intricate contours of nature has become the normative definition. While theologians may have ignorantly yielded the field to experimental science in basic matters of ontology, the partisans themselvs of science have come to judge that, in Toulmin's words, "it is a mistake to put questions about the reality or existence of theoretical entities too much in the centre of the

---

[18] For a discussion of theology as "imaginative construction" see Gordon Kaufman, *An Essay on Theological Method* (Missoula, MT: Scholars Press, 1975) and *The Theological Imagination* (Philadelphia: Westminster Press, 1981); for an account of the "fictive" character of theological reflection see Lonnie Kliever, "Polysymbolism and Modern Religiosity," *Journal of Religion* 59 (1979): 16994; see also Sallie McFague, *Metaphorical Theology* (Philadelphia: Fortress Press, 1982).

[19] Stephen Toulmin, *Foresight and Understanding: An Enquiry into the Aims of Science* (New York: Harper & Row, 1961), p. 109.

picture."[20] Indeed, science itself may be doing little more than acknowledg-
ing after a heady century or more of cognitive absolutism its own humble
seventeenth century origins. As a variety of historians have shown lately,
modern experimental science began during the age of Newton as a self-
consciously fallible reckoning of the natural world and as an implicit adoration of the Deity, an extension of the Calvinistic *theologia gloriae*.[21]

A second important development in science over the last decade figures
heavily here. We have in mind the effective marriage of physics with religious
thought in the subject area of quantum mechanics—what has popularly come
to be designated as "the new physics."[22] Quantum physics, which has begun
to press its influence across the full terrain of the natural sciences, has within
its own declared procedures purged the last remaining pretenses of any
descriptive finality. As physicist Fred Wolf has written, "the price of determinism is too high . . . the world from the view of quantum physics] is
already paradoxical and fundamentally uncertain."[23] The uncertainty of observation, combined with a profound tentatativeness for all scientific posits,
yields a portrait of the "new science" as having the same quasi-theological
character as its seventeenth century forbears. The new science, moreover,
has acquired a penchant for cosmic conjectures and religious analogies that
would make a hardened positivist quail. Hence, *scientia* has been combined
with religious reflection once again, although the impetus on this occasion
has come from the side of the former. Rather than merely taking cursory
notice of this situation, we should conclude that it is possible again to speak
theologically in the classical style with a gaze toward the universe at large
and that we should not to have to cower, as we have often done throughout
the present era, in a self-imposed ghetto of existentialist "resolve", or mere
subjectivist frippery.

A distinct caveat, however, should be entered here. A rapproachment
between science and theology should not necessarily be tied to the familiar
subterfuge in which certain religious thinkers use the models and metaphors
of the scientific world to make their own brief. The point is stressed by
Toulmin. "When we put scientific terms to non-scientific uses," insists

[20] Stephen Toulmin, *The Philosophy of Science* (New York: Harper & Row, 1960), p. 138.

[21] Two recent works in this vein worth mentioning are Barbara J. Shapiro, *Probability and
Certainty in Seventeenth-Century England* (Princeton, NJ: Princeton University Press, 1983)
and Frank E. Manuel, *The Changing of the Gods* (Hanover, NH: University Press of New
England, 1983).

[22] There are, of course, numerous titles pertaining to the new physics that have been
published since the mid-1970s. The most prominent are Fritjof Capra, *The Tao of Physics*
(Boulder, CO: Shambhala, 1975); Paul Davies, *Other Worlds* (New York: Simon & Schuster,
1980); Paul Davies, *God and the New Physics* (New York: Simon & Schuster, 1983); Fred Wolf,
Taking the Quantum Leap (New York: Harper & Row, 1981); Heinz Pagels, *The Cosmic Code*
(New York: Simon & Schuster, 1982).

[23] Wolf, pp. 204–5.

Toulmin, "the chief merit of a scientific approach is lost. For all that experiment or observation can show, one scientific myth is as good as another."[24] Such a propensity, unfortunately, has become increasingly widespread in the last twenty years with the spate of new books about the "new physics" and the "new biology." The majority of these works have not too concealed religious and metaphysical motives. Authors treating the new physics have been most forward in advancing such a cause, inasmuch as they have almost en bloc succeeded in convincing their lay audience that quantum mechanics corroborates some version of Eastern theosophy. This common, but highly tendentious, brand of Heisenbergian "metaphysics" derives historically from physicist Eugene Wigner's deduction that that experimental determination of an array of probabilistic "eigenstates" in all quantum mechanical interactions can be ascribed to the action of the hidden variable of "consciousness." In other words, the scientific observer's mind influences the outcome of an experiment.

Karl Popper, on the other hand, has convincingly shown that the selection of eigenstates—what is also known in technical parlance as "the reduction of the wave packet" or "the collapse of the state vector"—can be explained as readily in terms of "objective" subquantal processes as it can by the concept of observer dependence.[25] Hence, the interplay between the scientific perspective and the theological endeavor should not lead to another wallow in what Toulmin dubs "natural theology."

It is Toulmin's view that all attempts at natural theology, or "theological naturalism," were turned back by David Hume two hundred years ago, and the persent campaign to revamp a discredited argument by appeal to the tacit "spiritual" qualities of the new science is tantamount to intellectual dishonesty. We must agree with Toulmin within limits here. Whereas the relativization of the physical world picture that has transpired nearly without notice inmost philosophical and theological precincts does strongly contribute to a prospective new mutual respect among both scientists and theologians, such fertile exchanges should not be compromised by the hoisting anew of metaphysical petards. Theological discourse can be fortified by a fresh understanding of the scientific concern for stalling the more absurd epistemological options. The insouciant disregard on the part of twentieth century theologians for standards of intellectual rigor and a willingness to traffic in the culturally marginal and the purely fanciful has been lethal. Now that science itself has been cut down a notch in its own ontological allegations, the way is open for theological thinking to become more exact, methodologically franchised, and serious.

---

[24] Stephen Toulmin, *The Return to Cosmology* (Berkeley, CA: University of California Press, 1982), p. 32.

[25] See Karl Popper, *Quantum Theory and the Schism in Physics* (Totowa, NJ: Rowan & Littlefield, 1982).

We do not need a new natural theology, but we are obliged to bring the study of "nature" once more back into the arena of theological investigation. Nature must be viewed, again perhaps as it was among both Catholic and Protestant Scholastics; as a compendium of signs, as a veritable wealth of *vestigia*, of the divine wisdom. The same attitude wherein the study of nature per se is intuitively construed as an experimental subdiscipline of theological work can be found among the great seventeenth century minions of intellect who both shaped and sharpened what we now refer to blasely as the "scientific spirit." For instance, it was John Locke himself who declared that "the works of nature are contrived by wisdom, and operate by ways too far surpassing our faculties to discover or capacities to conceive, for us to be able to reduce them into a science."[26] And it was Newton who confessed in his sunset years that he saw all his own scientific achievements as but a few pebbles plucked from the seashore "whilst the great ocean of truth," he said, "lay all undiscovered before me." The original nisus of science has been theological all the way from Thales to Schroedinger. The fundamental difference between scientific statements and theological discourse is that the latter in the modern setting has remained referentially open, if not somewhat whorish in its choice of clients, whereas the former has often drifted toward its own version of iron dogmatism and apodicticity. The previous parting of modern science from theological thinking can be reckoned less to the native divergence of the two fields of knowledge than from the overweening (some might even be so bold as to say "totalitarian") authority granted mechanistic science by the intellectual community ever since LaPlace disposed of the God "hypothesis."

But the totalitarian sovereignty of mechanism has been greatly weakened since the advent of the quantum era, and it is reserved for theology to restore the traditional links that were so obvious three hundred years earlier. On the other hand, theology must not merely be exploited as a muff for our so-called "New Age" synthetically contrived theosophy—and sophistry. Science is no more a cipher for mysticism than theology is for the magical. As E. A. Burtt in his classical historical account has shown, the "metaphysics" of modern science is decidedly Christian and, in an extended manner of speaking, Biblical.[27] Thus the rehabilitation of theological discourse demands that the re-enthronement of science be accompanied by a respect for the cognitive precedence of Scripture on which the tradition of theology has been erected.

Ironically, however, the eclipse of theological thinking in the last twenty years may be imputed to a significant misreading of the relationship between the heritage of Biblical religion and what has come to be termed within our

---

[26] John Locke, *Some Thoughts Concerning Education*, 190.

[27] Edwin Burtt, *The Metaphysical Foundations of Modern Science* (Garden City, NY: Doubleday, 1954).

argot as the "secular." The view that the submergence of thought in secularity could be traced directly to the Yahwistic faith of the Hebrews was as much the gravemen of trendy theology in the 1960s as the obsession with the history of religions and "pluralism" is today.[28] This particular view had its genesis in neo-Orthodoxy, and it can be abridged with hindsight into the following set of propositions:

(1) Faith in the Biblical Deity who rules history and judges all human projects and institutions means that even ecclesiastical claims, theological norms, and personal credos are "relativized."

(2) Our modern historical flux and deracination of values is the immediate outgrowth of the Biblical outlook.

(3) Therefore, the wholehearted embrace of our secular, "godless" world is the *de rigeur pose* of informed theologians.

Consider, for example, Gilkey's assertion that "we are immersed in historical and social process; and here our lives, for good or ill, are led."[29] Such an opinion can be taken as the logical outcome of the old, Barthian transcendentalism in which eternity and time were radically discrepant from each other. In the absence of any meaningful reverence for what is "wholly other," the completely familiar or fully immanent comes to take on its own sacral structure. This total axiological reversal of the now deceased neo-orthodox piety has overspread liberal theology like a cirrus haze since the 1960s. And it explains in part why the typical Niebuhrian affirmation of "loyalty to the One" suddenly changed into an untrammeled celebration of the diverse and transitory. In a strange sort of alchemy the neo-orthodox moment of theological eminence became *mutatis mutandis* the instant of its dissolution.

Nevertheless, it is now the case that if the theological vocabulary is to have any intension whatsoever, the earlier Scriptural referents must be secured anew. For without its Scriptural foundation theology at best becomes an odd kind of literary critique; at worst it winds up a mouthpiece for trend mongers with no more substance or authority than popular journalism. Admittedly, it remains difficult to safeguard the prestige of Scripture when the text itself has been rigorously historicized by philology, sociology, and cultural anthropology. But our mounting fascination in the realm of Biblical investigation with sundry hermeneutics of suspicion should not impair recognition of the elemental truth that the amassing of historicist data actually has but a modest bearing on theological conversation. Research in antiquities is constantly revealing, by way of example, information pertinent to the *Sitz im*

---

[28] For example, consider Gilkey's statement made some time ago: ". . . it was just those elements affirmed by the early Church as a part of the Biblical view which, antithetical to the Hellenistic spirit, were to become the foundation of the modern modd we now call 'secular'." *Naming the Whirlwind: The Renewal of God-language* (New York: Bobbs-Merrill, 1969), p. 35.

[29] Langdon Gilkey, *Society and the Sacred* (New York: Crossroad, 1981), p. 103.

Leben of Plato's dialogues. Yet philosophers continue to treat the writings of Plato primarily with a philosophical and not with a historical regard. The same cautionary remark should be extended to theological thinking. If nineteenth century Teutonic scholarship uncovered both the wealth of historical life and the historicity of the faith tradition, it becomes a *reductio ad absurdum* nowadays to "divinize" history itself.

At the same time, both linguistic scrutiny and what might loosely be construed as contemporary *Religionswissenschaft* are by their own accord rekindling an appreciation for the more traditional Biblical transcendentalism. The anthropology of religious symbols, behavior, and forms—which with its profound sociologistic bias has had a lot to do with theology's failure of nerve—sought with out success to reduce Biblical faith to one among many ancient cultuses. What certain scholars steeped in the previously mentioned methodologies have shown, however, is that the Scriptural standpoint is not hermeneutically equivalent to, say, the ritual supplication of Shiva. Such an argument has been advanced by Herbert Schneidau, an historian of literature who is certainly not a theologian in the customary mode. After dissecting the Bible as text rather than as holy writ, Schneidau astonishingly concludes that we must guardedly impart some independence to "kerygma." He writes: "The kerygma is like a stand of wheat; deracinated and transplanted from its Near Eastern setting, it may hybridize and eventually flourish in nearly unrecognizable forms, far from its native place. We might say it travels well."[30]

Broadly speaking, the kerygma represents the theological formalism of Scripture. It does not belong to the pure textuality of Biblical writing toward which hermeneutical inquiry is explicitly aimed, but to the continuum of interpretation that manifests itself as "tradition." The kerygma, like the kingdom of God, transits within, but cannot be assimilated to, the "present eon." Ultimately, the historicization of Scriptural meaning must leave intact the kerygma. Hence, theological thinking is in the final analysis impervious to the process of relativization and radical enculturation, as has taken place since the "death of God" episode.

The reason for the proximate independence of theological discourse from radical enculturation, or from complete "secularization," is that from the very beginning its domain of reference has been that which surpasses the limits of all syntax, tradition, and modalities of culture. Contrary to even the most determined claims of "secular theology," the source and ganglion of the theological expedition is not located anywhere within the *saeculum*. So long as theological thinking continues to acknowledge that it has a patrimony which is Judeao-Christian (and, in truth, any serious argument to the contrary would prove synthetic and specious), it can never be finally absorbed in the prerogatives of pure historicism or an ungraded pluralism. In fine, if

---

[30] Herbert N. Schneidau, *Sacred Discontent: The Bible and Western Tradition* (Berkeley, CA: University of California Press, 1977), p. 304.

theological thinking is not to perish in the end from the modern siege of historico-relativizing criticism, which has now weakened perhaps from the recognition of its own metaphysical improprieties and methodological contradictions, it must like the assimilated ethnic at last renew respect for its own roots.

In short, theology must assent that it is in its own marrow and core a species of Biblical theology. And by "Biblical" theology we mean not an uncritical and quasi-doctrinaire deference to the surface grammars of ancient texts, as was the case with neo-orthodoxy, but a hermeneutically sophisticated endeavor to make larger sense of the contingencies of history, the multiplicity of our symbolic practices, and the vagaries of cultural transformation. For behind the phantasmagoric play of cognitive icons in what Sorokin would have termed our modern "sensate" culture still remains the Holy One, the "Ancient of Days," if we may employ the old, honorific tropes. Theology, therefore, never retreats from affirming the fundamental standpoint of "faith," which at the same time spurs an understanding that the divine reality outscripts all representations and "constructions".[31] A Biblically based theology is not a historical preservation project. It constitutes, according to Samuel Terrien, the "commemoration of presence . . . and the celebration of presence in the midst of the community of faith which extends from the theophanic past to the epiphanic end of history."[32] This worshipful, yet articulate and informed response to theophanic "presence," even today, genuinely grounds the theological enterprise. Whereas a conscious attention to the "scientific" character of the theological search, as we have seen, redeems the discipline from mystagogy and the more puerile conceits of "re-mythologizing", a fidelity to Scripture saves it from becoming a watered down sociologism, or simply bad anthropology.

Biblical "religion," as John Dominic Crossan has reminded us, is unique because it is "parabolic religion"—a religion whose language does not describe but *defies*, a religion in which God as presence rather than as "representation" is "given a little room in which to be God."[33] The obsession of much postwar theological writing has been with Tillich's "method of correlation" whereby, loosely paraphrased, the language of theology can be transmuted into human self-knowledge. However, it may be at last worthwhile for contemporary theologians to ponder again the statement of Calvin that "man never attains to a true self-knowledge until he has previously contemplated the face of God."[34]

[31] This is the essential argument that I have offered in *The Alchemy of the Word* (Missoula, MT: Scholars Press, 1979). It is also advanced by various authors in *Deconstruction and Theology* (New York: Crossroads, 1982).

[32] Samuel Terrien, *The Elusive Presence: The Heart of Biblical Theology* (New York: Harper & Row, 1978), p. 41.

[33] See John D. Crossan, *The Dark Interval: Towards a Theology of Story* (Niles, IL: Argus Communications, 1975), p. 76.

[34] John Calvin, *Institutes of the Christian Religion*, I, i, 2.

SECTION II

SCIENCE

CHAPTER 3

SCIENCE AND THE QUEST FOR "WISDOM"

"Wisdom is a kind of science in so far as it has that which is
common to all the sciences . . . But since it has something proper
to itself above the other sciences, in so far, that is, as it judges
them all, not only as to their conclusions, but also as to their first
principles, therefore it is a more perfect virtue than science."
—St. Thomas Aquinas

Perhaps the most formidable obstacle for theological thinking is the
epistemological challenge posed by modern science.

The canons of modern science, first set down by Francis Bacon in the
sixteenth century, were a sharp departure from the methods of demonstration and verification extolled in the Middle Ages. The late Medieval standpoint, however, was not criticized by early modern philosophers, as
textbooks often contend, only for its "metaphysical" approach toward dealing
with questions about nature. Late Medieval "Scholasticism" was saddled less
with a lack of empirical acumen than with an excessive dependence on
deductive logic as a tool for resolving critical issues. While Descartes is
customarily given credit for dismantling Scholasticism and rebuilding the
foundations of knowledge, the assault against the "barbarous" hegemony of
the Schoolmen was in full swing nearly three centuries earlier among the
Italian humanists, who preferred classical rhetoric to the Aristotelian syllogism.[1] In that respect the aims of the Renaissance writers can be likened to
the French post-structuralists, who are beginning to influence theological
discourse. Both in their own time sought to dispel the cloying fog of a
philosophy choked with propositional formalities and locutionary trifles, and
to advance instead a "literary" standard for exposition and discussion.

Renaissance letters contributed to the formulation of a distinctly "modern" sensibility, as Paul Oskar Kristeller, the esteemed historian of that
period, has pointed out.[2] Baconian "science," which sought to place natural

---

[1] See William Kneale and Martha Kneale, *The Development of Logic* (Oxford: The Clarendon
Press, 1962), p. 300.
[2] See Paul Oskar Kristeller, *Renaissance Thought: The Classic, Scholastic, and Humanist
Strain* (New York: Harper & Row, 1961), p. 22f.

philosophy on an experimental rather than a speculative footing, can also be reckoned as part of the patrimony of the Renaissance project.[3] Early modern science as well as humanism were, from the etiological standpoint, endeavors to rekindle the spirit of ancient naturalism, communicated through Greek and Latin texts that had not previously been available to the Christian West. Their foil was the abstract supernaturalism of the university facultites, which over the centuries had cultivated a theological dogmatics estranged from Scripture, an Aristotelian science that was based thoroughly on authority rather than observation, and a logicism that had little to do with inquiry into the environing world. Medieval thought had ossified because it had become totally dependent on the intellectual habits of the cloister. In the same vein the so-called post-modern movement in philosophy, linguistics, literary criticism, and religious thought can be construed as a revolt against the late modern version of "supernaturalism," the Russellian formalism that both transposed and eviscerated contemporary philosophy.

One curious outcome of Russelian formalism in twentieth century thought has been the mystique of the computer. Since its invention at the close of the Second World War the computer has inspired awe and anxiety, usually to excess, for one simple reason: it works not by force but by number. Like Plato's philosopher king, its sovereignty is impalpable, and therefore cannot be easily dislodged. The glorification of the power of number, and by extension the act of computation, harks back to the strange religiosity of the ancient Pythagoreans. But its veritable apotheosis belongs to the era we call the "modern." We find its first clear instance in the fourteenth century with Pico della Mirandola's proclamation in his *Oration on the Dignity of Man* of "a new method of doing philosophy—a method based on numbers."[4] But Pico's proclamation went decidedly against the sentiments of his age. It would take the Leibnizian metaphysics of unfolding monads—in itself a refinement of Pythagoras' metaphysics—to bring such numericism to a working fruition. And out of Leibniz' dream of a *mathesis universalis*, a world where the Medieval notion of change as the alteration of substance gave way to the dance of integers, sprung the vision of a formalist science which would much later become incarnate in the ENIACs and UNIVACs of the mid-twentieth century. From the beginning our cultural as well as philosophical ambivalence toward "technology" per se has been a case of collective psychological transference, an uneasiness about the soundness of Pico's bold new "method."

---

[3] Baconianism can best be understood in light of the rejection on scholastic logic and metaphysics on the part of the Italian humanists, who exercised an influence on English letters and thought.

[4] Pico della Mirandola, "Oration on the Dignity of Man," in Arturo B. Fallico and Herman Shapiro (eds.), *Renaissance Philosophy: The Italian Philsophers* (New York: The Modern Library, 1967), p. 163.

The cult of numericism, of course, found its crucial, philosophical expression in Russell's agenda for the reform of logic. Russell's endeavor to assimilate mathematics to logic, or with the theory of implication, was in itself a watershed for both science and philosophy. To the degree that Russell identified mathematical operations with the articulation of systems of "constructions" or formal relations, he was responsible for an important, but frequently overlooked, changeover in the tasks of modern inquiry. Since the seventeenth century the alliance of speculative mathematics with inductive science, first cemented in the Cartesian geometry, had pushed the ideal of a *mathesis* in the direction of the calculus of functions. Empiricism in natural philosophy was matched by an advanced algebraism in mathematical thinking. The Russellian reformation, which actually amounted to a convergence of trends and experiments that had been going on throughout the nineteenth century, resulted in what might be characterized as a renewed, "metaphysical"—perhaps even a mystical—grounding for the philosophy of number. The Pythagorean insistence that ultimate reality is the *monas* or "unity," which they opposed to "succession," "counting", or mere "arithmetic", has its correlation in Russell's dictum that all enumeration is properly understood as the classification of classes. Furthermore, the well-known silence of the ancient Pythagoreans concerning numerical secrets indicates a basic disinterest in the exoteric markers of human thought: what is essentially public, polysemic, grammatical, and communicable. Russell's development of the symbolic logic, through which the vagaries of natural semantics are winnowed into an invariant structure of propositional objects and entailments grasped by a circle of philosophically trained illuminati, can be taken as a modern version of the Pythagorean project.

But we must also remember that not only did this rigid formalization of the concept of number, coupled with the reduction of literacy to logic, make possible the science of programming. In addition, it conduced over time to the general habit of thinking about computing as an integral form of intelligence. Whereas the Athenians had regarded *techne* primarily as art, and thereby as something distinct and inferior when paired with philosophical knowledge, the rebirth of numericism in this century gave rise to a view of "technology" as the unfoldment of a deeply embedded universal structure. We find this outlook not only in such critics of technology as Jacques Ellul, but also in Heidegger. It is also visible in the writings of our so-called "futurists," who rhapsodize about technological change in the same way their Calvinist forbears expatiated on the goodness and providence of the Deity. The notion that technology is the outworking of a stratum of formal relationships, hitherto hidden behind the historical flux, can be seen as a kind of metaphysical similitude with the Russellian paradigm of logic. And the Russellian formalist paradigm has its own mundane analogy in the central processing unit of the computer, whose "machine language" transforms all inputs, whether they be operating instructions or bits of data.

Formalism as a style of thinking, however, has a far more trenchant significance than as an index to fashions in the imaging of technology. Following Heidegger's discussion, we may conclude that methodological formalism, or philosophical "rigorism" as it has sometimes been called, constitutes the very metaphysical angle of vision for the modern epoch. According to Heidegger, what in this day and age we refer to as "technology," at least in a non-technical manner, is not simply the ensemble of sophisticated equipment, control functions, processes, and instrumentalities which we observe in our everyday surroundings. A more precise term for such tangible machinery would be "technics." The "essence" of technology in Heidegger's interpretation is a peculiar "world view," which he calls "enframing." It is "modern science's way of representing" which "pursues and entraps nature as a calculable coherence of forces."[5] Technology is akin to thinking, inasmuch as it is a distinctive "mode of revealing." It is a way of presenting the "real," which in itself is a kind of presencing. In the "technological" mode of revealing the structure of reality is presented in such a way that the human subject contemplates only its own artifices. Technology is the mirror of human activity. In that respect, for Heidegger, the modern glorification of technological feats and activity is a colossal case of human narcissism. The slant of modern science is to manipulate and configure the world at hand, so that it appears only as an extension of human design and will, as an elaborate prosthetic. Yet through this act of "enframing" modern science and technology loses sight of what is hidden to both inquiry and thought. As Heidegger expresses the matter: "The threat to man does not come . . . from the potentially lethal machines and apparatus of technology. The actual threat has already affected man in his essence. The rule of Enframing threatens man with the possibility that it could be denied to him to enter into a more original revealing and hence to experience the call of a primal truth."[6]

Later in the same essay Heidegger calls for a return from scientific and technological thinking, which he identifies as "calculative", to the artistic outlook. The artistic perspective is a "poetic" one; it allows the real to be what it is to be, or in Heidegger's own innovative phraseology, it lets "the world world." The artist, says Heidegger, is intimately bound up with things as they manifest in their phenomenal or primordial state. The artist, unlike the scientific investigator or the technician, does not abstract from the concrete texture of experience and natural language in the pursuit of what the Greeks termed the pragmata. The artistic imagination is concerned not with the "form" of things, but with their "being," that is, with their relations and interconnections to what is as yet unmediated by explanatory models.

---

[5] Martin Heidegger, *The Question Concerning Technology and Other essays*, trans. William Lovitt (New York: Harper & Row, 1977), p. 21.

[6] *Question Concerning Technology*, p. 28.

Scientific thought in Heidegger's account is actually a truncation of "thinking" in the more basic sense, because it radically finitizes the aims as well as the rules of rational investigation. Heidegger's critique of science and technology, on the other hand, is really an indictment of formalism, not science at large. For, as we shall see, contemporary science has burst its own formalist fetters and embarked on a venture which does not diverge seriously from Heidegger's own formulation of thinking the unthought.

Heideggerrian philosophy does not serve well as a vehicle for overcoming the formalist impasse, however, because in showing up the limitations of numericism and deductive rationality, it leads us back into what might be termed "the occultist fallacy". The occultist fallacy means that truth and sensicality somehow must be divorced from the intelligibility of standard philosophical language. It was Heidegger's own suspicion of standard philosophical language that led him in his later years to develop a kind of hermetic poetry, rather than familiar expository discourse, in his writing. For Heidegger, *poesis* as opposed to *mathesis* requires the dissolution of the formal principle entirely in epistemology and semantics. The assimilation of science to art results in a kind of abstruse mystagogy, where the intellectual quest becomes a variant of what in the sixteenth century was dubbed "natural magic." Genuine theological thinking cannot appropriate wholesale Heidegger's "solution" to the formalist dilemma, because to take that step would be tantamount to leaping into the morass of estheticism, or at worst a gnostic illuminism. In his assault on the mathematicization of modern science, and by extension in the phenomenalism of post-Cartesian philosophy, Heidegger closes off the possibility, rightly understood in contrast by Hegel, that deductive formalism still belongs within the world's vast matrix of rationality. The Cartesian and Russellian projects are not to be dismissed out of hand, but revaluated in light of a more overarching or transcendental view of how numeric ontology is inseparable from linguistic reality, which in the tradition of the West have been under the propietorship of philosophy.

Much of the modern "warfare" between science and theology, or between science and traditional philosophy, can be construed as an internecine conflict between Pythagoreans and Platonists, or between the priests of number and the devotees of *logos*. The formalization of modern science had its origins in the need for precise navigational instruments and ballistic devices during the age of European mercantile expansion. It was, in fact, Galileo's own puzzlement over such everday, mechanical problems that spurred his efforts to redescribe physical motion in terms of mathematical trajectories and geometric regularities rather than Aristotelian entelechies. The problems themselves, Galileo attested, were to be discharged through "the force of rigid demonstration such as occur only in mathematics."[7] Thus

---

[7] Galileo Galilei, *Dialogues Concerning Two New Sciences*, trans. Henry Crew and Alfonso de Salvio (New York: Dover Publications, 1954), p. 276.

the progressive mathematicization of the sciences from the seventeenth century onwards can be explained in part as a general effort to make the scheme of philosophical rationality congruent with the praxis of disciplined inquiry. This new philosophical rationality at the same time was conceived not as a subordination of theory to practice, or in Heidegger's terms of disinterested contemplation to a calculating subjectivity, but as fresh discovery of the intelligible patterns wrought within nature by the Creator himself. In sum, in the early modern context science and theology were far more coordinated than we are wont to suspect.[8]

A plea to recover this early modern perspective can be found in the works of the contemporary, neo-Calvinist theologian Thomas F. Torrance, who ironically has made a far more persuasive case for the unity of scientific and theological thinking than has occurred in the liberal camp. Science serves to highlight the signatures of divinity, for Torrance, because natural laws themselves "may be regarded as empirical sequences and regularities, symmetries and invariant relations which God has imparted to nature admidst all the changes and varieties of its contingent processes," but also can be understood "by reference to the legislative Word and unifying Rationality of God the Creator and Sustainer of the universe."[9] Torrance's unique contribution to contemporary theological conversation has been his adherence to the classic Augstinian/Protestant doctrine of God's unconditional freedom and sovereignty while allowing for the intimate presencing of the Creator within the created order. In that respect Torrance's position can be grasped as a skillful synthesis of the neo-orthodox demand for divine transcendence with the modernist interest in reconciling dogma and empirical knowledge. Furthermore, Torrance's conception of "thinking" incorporates Heidegger's emphasis on probing concealed relations within the phenomenal realm whie remaining inside a theistic frame of reference. "In proper theological thinking," writes Torrance, "we have to break through the surface to the depths of intelligible reality and engage with orderly relations lodged in it that reach out far beyond our experience and understanding, that is to say, with patterns that have objective depth and which cannot be identified with the surface patterns of our formal logic or phenomenal motifs." Theological activity is not an ancillary, subsidiary or "meta-" activity, as the modernist argument would have it, but a true foundational undertaking of human reason which "must be regarded as a whole in accordance with our intuitive

---

[8] The two classic studies of this phenomenon are Basil Willey, *The Seventeenth Century Background* (New York: Doubleday, 1955) and Basil Willey, *The Eighteenth Century Background* (Boston: Beacon Press, 1940). Also see inter alia Leah Jonas, *The Divine Science* (New York: Octagon Books, 1973); Paul H. Kocher, *Science and Religion in Elizabethan England* (San Marino, CA: The Huntington Library, 1953); Robert K. Merton, *Science, Technology and Society in Seventeenth Century England* (New Jersey: Humanities Press, 1970).

[9] Thomas F. Torrance, *Christian Theology and Scientific Culture* (New York: Oxford University Press, (1981), p. 123.

apprehension of the whole pattern of Truth."[10] Torrance's defense of what might be termed the "omnidisciplinary" concern of the theological enterprise is not the outcome of some sort of panlogist metaphysics, but his understanding of the responsibility of Christian reflection in view of a most profound reading of the Incarnation.

In Torrance's interpretation of the formative period of Christian theology, the recognition by the faithful that God had dwelt fully in his Son, a historical personality, and continued to abide through his Holy Spirit, led to the crystallization of the belief in the Holy Trinity, which ultimately became established as the "metaphysical" idea of *perichoresis*, or the mutual interpenetration of the divine persons in the Godhead. The notion of *perichoresis*, says Torrance, ineluctably entails an "onto-relational" outlook on how we must conceive Deity. The perichoretic standpoint requires that the divine mystery and action is to be sought, not only in the sphere of personal and historical redemption, as Reformation pietism sought, but in the natural order as well. Moreover, genuine theological thinking, which forms the backdrop for an anticipated "theological science," is contingent upon the concurrent ordering and reciprocal intercalation of the different areas of proper inquiry. For Torrance, the onto-relational standpoint in science draws us out of the paradigm of classical mechanics into the world view of quantum physics, which composes the subject matter for the chapters immediately following.[11]

As we shall see in subsequent discussions, the Trinitarian conception furnishes a scaffolding for the whole tri-partite constellation of theological thinking. The doctrine of the first Person, "Father" or Maker of the world, leads to a "natural theology" in which the origin of those things manifest and intelligible can be traced to a unitary source. The doctrine of the second Person, "Son" or Redeemer, implies the radical task of "hermeneutics," the descent into the unknown and uncharted following Hegel's metaphor of the Golgotha of Absolute Spirit. The doctrine of the third Person, Holy Spirit or Sustainer, means the compression of all historical artifacts and textual meanings into the mode of "revelation." An account of the significance of the second Person yields not simply a Christology and a soteriology in the orthodox sense, but what we shall describe as a *bathotheology*—a theology of Hegel's "depths of Spirit," the unsurveyed psycho-historical terrain of the

---

[10] Thomas F. Torrance, *Theological Science* (New York: Oxford University Press, 1969), p. 129.

[11] Torrance writes that the "perichoretic relation" in the Patristic era "was reached through a movement of thought that took its rise from the empirico-theoretical ground of the incarnational activity of God within the spatio-temporal structures of our world, and it remains, indirectly through the level of the economic trinitarian relations, empirically correlated with that ground . . . Hence it would not be surprising if a perichoretic relation, with appropriate and adequate change in relation to the nature of the subject-matter in the field, could be applied to the problem of quantum theory or of particle theory." *The Ground and Grammar of Theology* (Charlottesville, Va.: University of Virginia Press, 1980), p. 176.

human eon, the penumbra of silence and unspoken resonance surrounding the language of religion.

If natural theology, or Creator-theology, issues in an appraisal of the divine codings within what has classically been called "nature", bathotheology urges us to consider what lies behind and "beneath" those surface emblems. The objective of bathotheology is not unlike so-called "depth psychology" with the exception that it does not posit the existence of a "collective unconscious" or a transpersonal "psyche", a set of constructions which makes such a method a metaphysics in its own right. Bathotheology, at least from the linguistic standpoint, remains within the ambit of traditional dogmatics. But at the same time it overreaches the boundaries of dogmatics in bursting the very, classical form of theology. In that respect it signifies theology's ending. And finally a proper understanding of the role of the third Person of the Trinity brings us to the threshold of the infinite presence and active "rule" of the One who has in the testimony of faith been known as God, Yahweh, the Almighty, or the Lord of all.

But returning to the question of the interrelation between scientific and theological thinking, we are invited to ask whether the historical conflict between the two intellectual constituencies has not been perhaps a slightly specious one.[12] It may be in fact that the untold labors since the eighteenth century to "reconcile" modern science with religious ideas, or to secure a "scientific" grounding for the theological project, has been a lot of spluttering and spittle. Scientific thinking, as Toulmin has repeatedly emphasized, has a built-in disposition that can only be called contingent and relativistic. Moreover, Toulmin notes, rather than actually superseding the "myths" of classic Christianity, modern science has been engaged in its own version of *mythopoeisis*. The twentieth century doctrine of evolution, for example, has functioned more like a rival faith system than a rational alternative to the older Judeao-Christian cosmology. It has been a "scientific myth," according to Toulmin, but a myth nonetheless.[13]

However, the basic difference between modern scientific mythology and what is best described as the "classical" outlook, the grand synthesis of the Hebraic and Hellenic world pictures that reached maturity in the thirteenth century, is not so much one of substance as one of respective starting points,

[12] A classic treatment of this contention is Andrew Dickson White, *History of the Warfare of Science with Theology* (New York: D. Appleton, 1925).

[13] If we compel astronomy and physics, says Toulmin, "to serve us with a revised version of Genesis and Revelation we dig a pit for ourselves." *The Return to Cosmology: Postmodern Science and the Theology of Nature* (Berkeley, CA: University of California Press, 1982), p. 52. Langdon Gilkey has gone even further to argue that modern science has in essence served to "purify" the language of myth. According to Gilkey, scientific and religious discourse belong together as part of the fundamental epistemological template of a given culture. Theology reflects on the internal meanings of this culture, which includes its scientific outlook. Langdon Gilkey, *Religion and the Scientific Future: Reflections on Myth, Science, and Theology* (New York: Harper & Row, 1970), p. 65ff.

a signal fact which Toulmin overlooks. The modern scientific "revolution" did not originate strictly as a more plausible narrative concerning the behavior of natural phenomena, of which there were countless, competing varieties during the late Renaissance. It decidedly came about through a reformation of "method." The preoccupation with method, or the route of formal procedure for drawing theoretical conclusions, was the smoldering spark, as we well know, that ignited the Cartesian vision. And Francis Bacon, who is popularly albeit wrongly credited with pioneering the new approach of what was then known as "natural and experimental philosophy," wrote in his *Novum Organon* not a treatise on scientific induction as much as a set of regulae, or precise rules, for the ordering of human experience. Bacon's "method," therefore, was really an assault on all forms of idealism, apriorism, and authoritarianism which started from received notions, derogatorily tagged "idols," and moved through consideration of given data to what could easily be regarded as foregone conclusions. In Bacon's memorable simile, the "true method of experience" is to first light the candle and then show the way.[14] In contrast, the classic tradition to which Bacon was reacting centered on the method of deductive generalization, commencing with a universal and established truth and progressing toward its confirmation in sense particulars. We find the warrant for this method clearly enunciated by Aristotle in the opening of the *Physics*. All genuine knowledge, for Aristotle, is founded on "acquaintance with principles." Principles are in themselves lucid and distinct notions, which convoke agreement, and which therefore can be utilized to explore more obscure regions of natural knowledge. The method of the "science of nature" is to "commence with things that are more obvious and knowable and then to proceed in the direction of that which is more evident according to nature."[15] The Baconian innovation was to challenge the assumption that clarity and consensus equalled veracity. The mysteries of nature cannot be rationalized, even if done so elegantly, in terms of ancient philosophical formulas, or the wisdom of the schoolteachers. Nature must be respected in its own guise and presentation. Bacon's method of "experiment" thus was not far from the use of "bracketing" demanded by later phenomenologists, except of course that the *Novum Organon* had a sharp eye toward the practical benefits to be garnered by humanity, if science were at last liberated from the restraints of antique "authority."

The "method" of Baconian science, which would later be translated into the philosophy of empiricism, had far more strength in the nascent war with religion than its world view. Bacon, after all, was quite a devout Anglican. And we must ask whether it has not been method, as opposed to "cosmology" or "scientific myth" in Toulmin's sense, which was, and in certain

[14] Francis Bacon, *Novum Organon*, lxxxii. See Edwin A. Burtt (ed.,), The English Philosophers from Bacon to Mill (New York: The Modern Library, p. 57.
[15] Aristotle, *Physics*, I, 184a.

measure remains, the occasion for the ongoing struggle between science and theology. In an important sense the problem today is not a clash of outlooks, inasmuch as both scientific and theological thinking have within the last few centuries adjusted quite dramatically their sights toward the natural order. The issue, in fact, is one of method. For what elementary school children recognize as "scientific method" has had a broad-reaching effect on the manner in which basic human experience and knowledge is converted into an acceptable intellectual consensus. Theological method—both in this century and in the more remote past—has tended to be just as rigorous as its scientific counterpart. The difference has consisted in the starting point as well as the peculiar yield of inferences.

For example, Bacon's experimentalism can be seen as an effort to derive philosophical truth from an attention to the vicissitudes and potencies of nature. Indeed, the entire bent of early modern science, if scholars such as Frances Yates and Charles Schmidt can be taken forthrightly, was closely intertwined with the practice of erudite occultism, and in its initial stages could be looked upon, according to Brian Vickers, as a "rival magic."[16] Yates' epochal thesis was that the preoccupation of such Renaissance "magi" as John Dee and Cornelius Agrippa with astrology and numerology, along with their Kabbalistic belief that arithmetic relations formed the hidden fabric of the universe, paved the way for the mathematicization of scientific investigations into nature. Various scholars, influenced by the Yates argument, have espied the indelible imprint of Renaissance magic on scientific reasoning, particularly in the seventeenth century. The analogies without dispute extend to Bacon. Bacon's very advocacy of "experiment" can be interpreted in this light, because among the magis themselves the word did not mean a disinterested and laborious process of testing the behavior and properties of bodies or substances; it referred to an occult ritual of conjuring up concealed forces or elements. Baconian "method", therefore, was actually a careful refinement of the magical attitude itself. In the Renaissance the magical attitude, permitted to flower by the re-paganized Italian curia, contributed to a redirection of "science" itself away from heavenly matters toward tellurian secrets and the production of worldly assets. Modern science was an outgrowth of this redeployment of method, which no longer sought to unfold the mysteries of divine intervention from on high, but rather to convoke the immanent forces operating from below.

Yet in contrast with contemporary neo-paganism, the Renaissance magi/

---

[16] See the introduction to Brian Vickers (ed.), *Occult and Scientific Mentalities in the Renaissance* (Cambridge: Cambridge University Press, 1984), p. 42. Other works that offer discussions in this vein are Francis Yates, *The Rosicrucian Enlightenment* (London: Routledge & Kegan Paul, 1972; Charles Schmitt, "Reappraisals in Rennaisance Science," *History of Science* 16 (1978): 200–14; R. S. Westman and J. E. McGuire, *Hermeticism and the Scientific Revolution* (Los Angeles: 1977).

scientists were generally devout Christians, who believed that the inferior workings of nature must incontrovertibly be perceived as part of the superior plan and governance of God Almighty. Originally scientific method was a special case of theological inquiry. To employ our own phraseology, we might say that the early modern period, in which science and theology were still part of the same cultural distillate, understood with a sensitivity that has long passed us by that theological thinking must probe to the depths as well as ascend to the heights. The vision had already been captured in the poetry of Dante. And it found its conceptual champions in the Renaissance, whose elaborate discourse—which was primarily literary and panegyrical in its content—is now but a historical curiosity. The Enlightenment, often construed as a second Renaissance, was responsible for a quite distinct outcome, insofar as it contributed to the rupture of theological and scientific modes of inquiry. It was the eighteenth, not the sixteenth, century that came forth with an unprecedented type of dogmatic thought to be known as "naturalism," which in turn engendered the haughty tradition of scientism so repugnant to twentieth century theologians and humanists alike. When science was shorn of its theological dimension, it became the "pale" and "cock-crow" positivism that Nietzsche disparaged. When theology became divorced from science, it stumbled into a shallow sort of religious experientialism, or the bloodless verbiage of a refurbished orthodoxy, from which it could no longer preserve its own innovative edge.

A new context for the rapprochment of scientific and theological thinking, however, has been laid in the waning decades of this century with the development of the science of quantum mechanics, or quantum theory. It is an ironic twist that the initiative for such a possible reunion has come from scientific circles, and not from the theologians themselves. One reason for this default may be simply that even a modest scientific literacy, notwithstanding a cursory familiarity with popular commonplaces about science, has not been a significant priority of theologians in the past twenty years. The theological mind unfortunately has been bewitched by the prestige of literary method, as well as the metaphoric model of the world, which easily conduces to the conclusion that religious truth invariably is either "socially constructed," privately nurtured, or cognitively uncompelling. Long ago the theological mind surrendered the premise that cosmology at large, or natural events written small, were suitable subjects for examination. Yet the enfranchisement of the theological point of view in the discussion of all matters, greater or lesser, was the abiding assumption of Christian thinkers well up into the eighteenth century. At present, theological writers, especially of a conservative stripe, cling to the stance of "faith" over against what is considered the idolatrous posture of scientific reckoning. But a faith which lacks an "understanding" that either refuses, or is incapable, of plumbing the depths of the world is a tawdry one indeed. For the church fathers at least, the output of an enlivened, inquiring faith was the classic ideal of "wisdom," tempered by the prophetic notion that the infinite mind of God always outstrips the finite pretensions of humanity. Wisdom, which is God's own oblique nature, encompasses what is hidden to the unregenerate intellect. According to Clement of Alexander, wisdom suffuses the entire universe and manifests itself in all forms of knowledge and praxis, whether they be art, philosophy, or experimental science. "The way of truth" is one and all, Clement argued.[17]

The "quantum era" of thinking, as we shall discern in the next chapters, opens up the radical possibility that such a view of the divine wisdom may be available to us once again after almost two millenia, albeit under a different nomeclature and syntax. The quantum perspective itself suggests that behind the totality of formal understanding, or the many units or "quanta" of perceptible reality, lies a mysterious intelligibility and symphony of activity. Quantum physics has itself probed into the deepest interlacings of the microcosmic order to lay bare the astounding sophia within all things. Yet it remains within the ambit of the macrocosmic science of universal, natural law. Before we make such inferences, on the other hand, we must survey briefly the history and implications of the quantum world picture itself.

---

[17] See H. B. Timothy, *The Early Christian Apologists and Greek Philosophy* (Assen, Netherlands: Van Gorcum & Company, 1973), p. 60.

CHAPTER 4

QUANTUM PHYSICS AS A NEW MODEL OF THINKING

"The quantum theory . . . presents us with a very great challenge,
for we are at all interested in such a venture, for in this theory
there is no consistent notion at all of what the reality may be that
underlies the universal constitution and structure of matter."
—DAVID BOHM

The birth of quantum thinking occured at the very close of the nineteenth century, on the 18th of May in the year 1899. On that day Max Planck,
who struck the word "quantum" into our vocabulary, presented some rather
unconventional and disturbing ideas to the Prussian Academy of Sciences.
Although these ideas would within a decade be dwarfed with respect to their
"revolutionary" impact by Einstein's theory of special relativity, which con-
centrated on the speed of light rather than its makeup, they caused ferment
in modern physics that would eventually explode into an altogether new
conception of the universe. The lecture in which Planck launched the
quantum era was quite torpid and erudite. "It should be of some interest,"
Planck commented, "that use of the two constants a and a' which occur in the
equation for radiative entropy offers the possibility of establishing units for
length, mass, time, and temperature which are independent of specific
bodies or materials and which necessarily maintain their meaning for all time
and for all civilizations, even those which are extraterrestrial and nonhuman,
constants which therefore can be called 'fundamental physical units of measurement.'"[1]

The two "fundamental units of measurement" were later compacted into
a single value denoted as h and christened "Planck's constant." Planck's
famous formula for radiation $E = h\nu$ (where "E" means energy and the Greek
letter "ν" indicates the wave frequency) came to be the lodestone for quantum mechanics in the same fashion as $E = mc^2$ proved to be the ballast beam
of relativity theory. Einstein's formula was the basis of the miraculous insight
that matter and energy are convertible. Such a discovery made possible the
harnessing of nuclear power. The far-flung ramifications of Planck's findings

---

[1] *Philosophical Magazine* 49 (1900):539–40. Quoted in Armin Herman, *The Genesis of Quantum Theory*, trans. Claude W. Nash (Cambridge, MA: The MIT Press, 1971), p. 11.

are less obvious, but equally momentous. Classical physics, which had arisen on the scaffolding built by Galileo, Descartes, and Newton, presupposed the uniformity of matter and energy. When Galileo wrote in his *Dialogues* that he assumed "matter to be unchangeable and always the same," he was voicing the underlying metaphysical prejudice of modern science. The establishment of the atomic theory of matter in the nineteenth century did not alter the classical scheme. Nor did the development of thermodynamics at the end of that century, where heat was interpreted as an effect of the random motion of molecules. The familiar and congenitally misunderstood concept of entropy was advanced as a leading feature of the thermodynamic model. Einstein subsequently showed that matter and energy were not always "conserved" in the strict sense of the term. The former could under extreme circumstances be transformed into the latter. Planck helped us recognize that matter and energy were not underlying and diffuse "substances". What we call "matter" and what we call "energy" are conditioned by certain *formal relationships*. These formal relationships are responsible for everything we experience in the universe. Such basic forms, which were first characterized numerically, Planck dubbed "quanta."

The inference as to the existence of quanta came about in much the same manner as Einstein's thesis that the velocity of light is the universal constant. Einstein set forth his doctrine of relativity in response to the failure of a crucial experiment by Michelson and Morley to exhibit the presence of the cosmic "ether", which nineteenth century physics premised as the medium through which light waves propagated, Einstein reasoned that the Michelson-Morley debacle was due to a fundamental misapprehension of the nature of light itself. And once that switch in assumptions had been made, the experimental data was no longer inscrutable or "anomalous." Likewise, Planck's suggestion of quanta was motivated by a schism between theory and empirical fact. The contradiction revolved around what was known as "black body radiation."

According to calculations made from the dominant theory of the day, energy, once it had been absorbed by a totally dark clump of matter, would quickly evaporate in a burst of high-frequency illumination. Such an event was ceremoniously baptized the "ultra-violet catastrophe." For, if the calculations were accurate, then all energy should have vanished from the material spectrum eons before. Clearly, that was not the case, and hence a rare crisis had befallen the physics of electromagnetism in much the same degree as the Michelson-Morley results buffeted classical dynamics.

One of the unswerving beliefs of nineteenth century physical science was the continuity of material processes. Regarding black body radiation, the postulate of continuity led scientists to the uncritical presumption that the disappearance of energy from matter must take place in an unimpeded stream. Planck, however, jiggled with numbers to prove that the ultra-violet catastrophe was avoided if energy escaped from matter in punctuated emissions or in discontinuous bursts.[2] These bundles of energy Planck named "quanta", which can be translated from the Latin to mean "things of small size or tiny quantities." Planck identified the basic quantum, nowadays referred to as "quantum of action," as equivalent to his primary unit h, an infinitesimally small amount. And the nub of Planck's equation was that all outputs of energy in the universe, whether at the submolecular level or in stellar magnitudes, must be some multiple of the quantum of action. Moreover, the factor for multiplying the basic quantum was the frequency for a wave of energy, that is, the number of oscillations per second. The higher the energy, the higher the frequency. Just as Einstein had made plain the reciprocity of matter and energy, Planck threw into relief the mysterious reciprocity of energy and *time*.

Such a connection was more than a mathematical convenience. It pried open philosophical doors and laid bare hidden passageways in the castle of metaphysics which had hitherto never been contemplated. Planck's quanta were immediately digested as simple, mathematical elements that could be invoked to explain the behavior of radiant energy. And they were soon appropriated by none other than Albert Einstein, a friendly adversary in successive decades to the new quantum theory, in order to explicate the so-called "photo-electric effect." Yet there was more. Material "particles" themselves could be seen as modes of quantized energy. The noted "Copenhagen" solution to the puzzle posed during the 1920s as to whether light should be depicted principally as a corpuscle (i.e., the "photon") or as a wave was adduced from quantum thinking. The Copenhagen interpretation advanced by Niels Bohr was essentially that light is both. The photon can wear two complementary disguises, depending on the experimental setting. Yet the Copenhagen verdict, which has disarmed scientific purists and enraged logicians, intimated that what we call "light"—or any type of electromagnetic energy as it turns out—is not a thing in itself. The discovery of the quantum of action, in keeping with which the propogation of energy must be viewed not as smooth but jerky, raised the interesting yet still not fully articulated possibility that everything that science inspects, tabulates, and correlates is really *form*. Form, or *information* in the more technical usage, constitutes the distribution of energy through time and space.

At the same time, we cannot separate energy from form, because such energy is always quantized or configured. The form or the description is not superimposed on something else, lending it any kind of meaning alone. It makes not sense to talk of a nebulous *tertium quid*, a ghostly real substance that comprises light apart from its manifestation as wave or particle. Light *is* a

[2] See Banesh Hoffman, *The Strange Story of the Quantum* (New York: Dover Publications, 1959), p. 16ff.

wave, and light *is* a particle. The confusion only intrudes, because we perhaps retain within our backbrains the primitive assumption that reality is a substratum upon which organization is imposed. The common sense of this viewpoint is a hoary as the Greeks and the search for the definitive substrate has meandered through an untold assortment of philosophical morasses. The philosopher Thales called such a substrate "water." Anaximander named it *apeiron* or the "indefinite." Plato characterized it as *ananke* or "necessity." Aristotle said all form interacts with "matter," which is *hyle* in Greek and connotes timber. Obviously, the metaphor of the sculptor carving his design from a block of wood nursed the Greek vision. Metaphysical speculation in its long-tenured career has emphasized both the substrate and the continuity of underlying reality. The controversy in the Western philosophical tradition between "idealists" and "materialist" has by and large been an issue of whether the forms or the substratum is considered to be ultimate somehow.

But in the quantum picture such a distinction, let alone a wrangle over which one should be accorded priority, becomes gratuitous. Form and matter become identical, and the question concerning which constituent is "real" and which is "illusory" happens to be as misplaced as asking whether the green cheese on the moon is Swiss or Edam. The quantized universe we inhabit can be compared in a crude way to a pointillist painting. Pointillism is the artistic technique, commercially utillized in printing the Sunday comics, by which the image arises by varying the density and spacing of tiny, monochrome dots. In fact, all photography relies on the same kind of application. Certain films are regarded as "grainy" if they evince the point-illist sleights of hand. The quanta are like these dots. But they must not be mistaken for "atoms" of energy, thereby smuggling in materialism through the laundry shoot. The quantum betokens the principle of limitation for all uniform entities. Red light, for instance, is different from green light, and visible light taken as a whole is different from microwaves, because all are different composites of the quantum of action, which in turn is the resultant of energy *and* time. In effect, the integration of quanta yields not "quantity" as both the derivation of the word and its mathematical formalism would suggest, but *quality*. They are what account for both form and the differentia-tion of forms in the cosmos.

Perhaps the most significant facet of the "quantum revolution has been the replacement of the antiquated concept of an observer versus an observed with the ironic ideal of what physicist John Wheeler has labelled "observ-ership." Observership means that it no longer makes sense to segregate subject and object or mind and nature.

The act of observation is really an interaction between what in the quantum lexicon are known as "conjugate variables." In order to understand the behavior of conjugate variables, we can think of a two-sided coin that is spinning upright on a table and wobbling in the direction of landing either heads or tails. While the coin is spinning we must judge that it is in an indeterminate state. Its final rest position has not been "decided" or transformed into actual information about the world. The final position, therefore, remains within the ambit of probability. These probabilities $p1$ and $p2$ are equally possible given the law of averages, so long as the coin's axis of spin is not yet listing. If we apply a force and tip the spin axis, the motion of the coin will collapse into a rest position of either heads or tails. Such a "decision" precludes the materialization of the other possibility. The heads and tails of the spinning coin are "conjugate" in the sense that they represent unique dimensions of the same phenomenon. On the other hand, the faces cannot be assimilated to each other; nor can they be reduced to the coin as an entirety. It would be ludicrous to conceive the coin without its faces as well as to define it in terms of, say, tails. Yet neither is it intelligible to speak of our "perception" of the total coin other than in an abstract idiom. We may have serial experiences of one side and then the other, but we can never examine the pair simultaneously. While the coin is spinning, it is permissible to state that heads and tails exist together; but this strange sort of "simultaneity" is lodged within the pouch of probability, or beyond the lens of direct awareness. The more that one of the "conjugate variables" tends toward finality or decision, the more the other recedes into uncertainty. If the coin flops down "heads," of course, we might object that it is equally certain it did *not* land tails. But that would be to make a semantic feint. We are using an illustration of an elementary binary choice for which we already have familiar terms to symbolize either outcome.

In the broader and exceedingly intricate universe which both science and philosophy are concerned we usually encounter alternatives, neither of which have ever been decided previously. The formulation of the problem of conjugate variables arose during the infancy of quantum physics, when it was pointed out, by Heisenberg in particular, that the position and momentum of a subatomic body like an electron could not be ascertained together. The conditions required for a precise reading of the value of the first function exclude an exact gauging of the second. A technical explanation of the reasons for this complication would demand more sentences that are practical here, and most popular works on the new physics reiterate the details of the so-called "uncertainty relations." What remains significant for our intentions is the recognition that the attainment of reliable knowledge has nothing to do, as our nineteenth century forbears assured themselves, with "seeing" the world as it is. The world "is" only in terms of the portion we confront and are inclined to examine.

On the other hand, there is a dynamic factor in the act of observation that cannot be communicated in the metaphor of the two-sided coin. The decision of the spinning coin as either heads or tails is the consequence of random falls brought about by the earth's gravitational field. The scientist's effort to locate an electron involves conscious attention; and it is this conscious attention which plays a pivotal role in quantum thought, so far as the discrimination of the particle's position is concerned. As the veteran adage goes: "to observe is to disturb." But why should observation precipitate a change in the quantum system, thereby undermining the strictly "objective" character of the phenomenon under scrutiny? Observation itself is like flicking the spinning coin with one's finger, thereby predisposing the end result. For several decades the influence of the scientific observer on the data of the experiment was construed in quantum mechanics as both a mathematical necessity and as an empirical truism. Yet the fundamental, more encompassing rationale for this effect was not given much serious philosophical reflection. Some books aimed at the public at large in the 1970s have made much ado about the creative and determining force of "consciousness" in negotiating the choice among quantum possibilities. Thus it is not surprising that certain enthusiasts would draw the wrong conclusions from scientific precepts and impart the suggestion that every experimenter is a kind of sorcerer or a fakir with supernatural aptitudes. Such leanings, even among old-guard partisans of the quantum position, to subjective idealism have incited a backlash among both scientific and philosophical traditionalists. No one would dare assail anymore the cogency of the quantum standpoint; but there are many who resist, sometimes violently, the unorthodox or non-mechanistic insinuations of the theory. Hence, we have the progression of Karl Popper, one of the twentieth century's most illustrious philosophers of science, that he wishes "to exorcize the ghost called 'consciousness' or the 'observer' from quantum mechanics, and to show that quantum mechanics is as 'objective' a theory as, say, classical statistical mechanics".[3] Mechanistic psychologists and philosophers have been trying for over a century to purge consciousness from scientific paradigms, to banish what Gilbert Ryle infamously branded the "ghost in the machine."

But consciousness cannot be liquidated. By the same token, we cannot reduce Wheeler's notion of "observership" to the personal propensities of the investigator. The upshot of quantum theory is that the observer disturbs, because the conscious aim of the experimenter constitutes a conjugate variable in the process of observation. Knower and known do not loiter at a distance from each other, like bashful teenagers at a high school dance. They interperetrate and shape one another. The more consciousness becomes skewed toward what is *not* consciousness (commonly denoted as the "objective" order), the more it takes on the garb of what is foreign to itself. Nineteenth century thinkers grasped this tendency of consciousness in elaborating the notion of "alienation," which indicates a state of mind wherein the individual envisages himself as the bald imprint of his outer environment. Conversely, the more consciousness folds back upon itself, the more it copies itself after its own inner anticipations. The extreme instance of this imbalance is autistic children, who have never engaged themselves with their external surroundings, and live in their own fantasy worlds, and schizo-

---

[3] Popper, p. 35.

phrenia in adults. Picture an electron that can delimit itself in terms of its own position or momentum without the intervention of a third party or "ideal observer." It would be as restricted as the ideal observer in specifying position and momentum simultaneously. For its "consciousness" per se can only span half of reality in a given instance. Conjugate variability may be expressed as the evolution of life toward consciousness, the basic rule of the universe that allows no being, such as Adam without Eve in the garden, to be complete in itself. To overcome this incompleteness it must interact with, or enter into the realm of, what is other to, yet intimately related to, itself. Yet in doing so it sacrifices both its integrity as well as its certainty of both itself and the not-self; and the product is *more consciousness*.

This rather tendentious metaphysical rendering of the quantum view of consciousness, worked out a century earlier by Hegel, has found surprising support in an abtruse demonstration called "Goedel's proof," otherwise titled the "incompleteness theorem." Kurt Goedel, Austrian mathematician and logician, tendered his proof in 1931. The proof was unfurled in an article called "On the Formally Undecided Propositions of the *Principia Mathematica* and Related Systems." The allusions to Alfred North Whitehead's and Bertrand Russell's *Principia Mathematica* was a telling one. For the agenda of the *Principia*, published two decades earlier, set the tone for the philosophical movement known as "logical positivism" which would overshadow much of Anglo-American thought between the wars. The project of the *Principia*, was to reduce mathematics to formal logic and to engineer an "ideal language" in which all propositions could be inferred from a system of axioms or rudimentary assumptions. Russell, especially, was a philosophical realist who held that logical statements corresponded to an independent order of things. Thus the tacit objective of the *Principia* was to excise all ambiguity from language, relativity from mathematics, and mystery from the cosmos. Descartes' dream of a *mathesis universalis*—a thoroughgoing and unqualified description of the world through the categories of number—and the nineteenth century aspiration to quantify all knowledge and science acquired a sophisticated platform in the early writings of Whitehead and Russell. Goedel, however, was able to flesh out the internal contradictions of the formalist program. Like all intellectual revolutionaries and critical geniuses, he did not meet his opponents cheek to jowl, but pricked them like a saddle-burr from within. Mechanistic science had gained its own non-theological version of Aquinas' *Summa Theologica* in the *Principia Mathematics*. Just as Aquinas solidified the primary articles of Medieval Christian faith by discerning a warrant for them in Aristotle, so the stolid cult of mechanism now found its justification in a mathematical metaphysics which would become the canon of a new *scientistic* "fundamentalism." But Goedel pointed up the way in which such a metaphysics could be upended.

Goedel's theorem contends that within any rigorous system of mathematics and logic there must necessarily be assertions, not to mention questions, that cannot be proven or disproven from the axioms of that system. If the system is self-consistent in the formally concise fashion demanded by Russell's logic, then it cannot express the entirety of reality. In short, such a system is *incomplete*. Similarly, if the system manages to be complete in the sense that it mirrors everything which is the case, it cannot be logically sound or self-consistent. As Ernest Nagel and James Newman have declared in their assessment of Goedel's accomplishments, there are "innumerable problems" in thought and mathematics "that fall outside the scope of a fixed axiomatic method, and that such engines are incapable of answering, however rapid their operations."[4] Goedel's demonstration may be the authoritative in-house refutation of the present "artificial intelligence" magisterium, who forecast that computer thinking will ultimately supplant the human mind. Formalists and mechanists have been drooling for centuries at the likelihood that certain manipulations of logical notations would eventuate in a definitive world description. The symbolic logic developed in the *Principia* was taken by many to be the long-awaited philosopher's stone that would transmute the dross of semantic ambiguity into the gold of syllogistic irrefutibility. But, alas, this occult fantasy was not to be consummated. In the words of Jacob Bronowski, Goedel confirmed that if "nature cannot be formalized," then scientific observation and deduction, which derives from abstract, *quantitative* rules and procedures, can only be said to approximate what is under study, no matter how inclusive or rigorous the concepts employed. Nature is always something "extra" in the dialogue of thought with its opposite. All axiomatic inference, according to Goedel are "self-referring." That is to say, they return to their own starting point; and anything they purport to "explain" is in the last analysis a clone of the presuppositions with which they began. A "complete" characterization of reality would bring the forth predicates that were not already contained in the subject. But then we would have an inconsistency not permitted within an axiomatic system in the first place. We might "know" certain facts, but they could not be "decisively" demonstrated.

When Einstein, together with his students Podolsky and Rosen came out with their famous paper (the "EPR statement") challenging quantum theory on the grounds that it was "incomplete," they were offering a back-handed compliment. For it has been the virtue of the quantum model that, in comparison with many of the ephemeral ideologies of the modern period, it has not pretended to supply the ultimate answer. Quantum theory insists on the illegibility of the master script of the universe. It shrinks from revelling in "mystery mongering," as many of its detrators have complained at intervals. But it does draw a gigantic question mark at the end of the

---

[4] Ernest Nagel and James Newman, *Goedel's Proof* (New York: New York: New York University Press, 1958), p. 100.

[5] Jacob Bronowski, *The Origins of Knowledge and Imagination* (New Haven, CT: Yale University Press, 1978), p. 80.

scientific sentence. The suggestion of "indeterminancy" at the heart of nature horrified even Einstein, who balked at the quantum paradigm until his dying day. *Herr Gott nicht würfelt* ("God does not play dice") he kept muttering against Heisenberg's gaggle of indeterminists in reference to the quantum supposition that all scientific results are statistical. What we experience is but the composite average of possible events or what are called "eigenstates" in the quantum parlance; it is never the complete and peerless "objective" happenstance that our common sense dogmas require. Einstein's own unspoken metaphysics was that of the seventeenth century Jewish philosopher Baruch Spinoza. Spinoza had envisioned a universe which was monolithic, unalterable, and governed by a rational necessity which could be conveyed through the methods of geometry. Indeed, Spinoza preferred his theological and ethical arguments in the guise of geometrical proofs. The mystique of geometrical certainty persisted even in the gestation of general relativity. Einstein shoved aside the Newtonian idea of gravity as a "force"; he reconceived it as the inherent "geometry" of space-time. Quantum theory blasted such geometrical determinism by showing there were knots, holes, kinks, and perspicuous irregularities in the space-time fabric. These irregularities accounted for the fact of indeterminism. John Wheeler would later coin the phrase "geometrodynamics" in which the fabric became an undulating "quantum foam" riddled with tiny "singularities" that constantly upset the coherence of nature. But, to paraphrase the ancient Greek poet, uncertainty was king, having cast out Zeus. The Deity may not have been proven to be a gambler, but he was at least a shrewd gamesman. In the coy phrasing of David Finkelstein, "if a complete world description exists in some Platonic sense, it is unavailable to us, and God plays with marked cards: He can read the backs, we cannot!"[6]

We cannot read the backs because our intellect is bounded. Divine wisdom, according to our religious traditions, comprises the infinite. The pretentions of modern scientism, which spins its principles and axioms from human understanding, to inviolable authority in its method, if not its conclusions, has been merely another timely episode in finite humanity's conspiracy to enclose the infinite. The Greeks named this drive to overstep cosmic limits *hubris* and saw it as the stuff of tragedy. Christian theology branded it *superbia* or the "sin of pride," which Augustine in his *The City of God* identified as the bacillus of all terrestrial conflict. Quantum theory recognizes the same *law of incompleteness* in the correlation of knowledge and experience with primary concepts. Goedel's proof displays how the law of incompleteness need not be only drawn inductively from the sorts of experimental problems incurred through the measurement of subatomic events; it also highlights the manner in which such a law is etched into the very codices

---

[6] David Finkelstein, "Quantum Logic and Quantum Mappings," in A. R. Marlow (ed.), *Quantum Theory and Gravitation* (New York: Academic Press, 1980), p. 81.

of language and thinking. When Kant in the preface to his *Critique of Pure Reason* asserted he was "abolishing reason to make room for faith," he was posing with hyperbole what might be the hidden agenda not just of post-modern reflection, but the quantum revolution as well. If there can be such a specimen as a "quantum faith," however, it is not blind acquiescence to dogmatic propositions such as were assailed by our seventeenth century precursors. Such a quantum faith is nothing more than the deep-felt conviction that the universe is forever open and that even the most platinum-plated lemmas of scientific conversation are refundable.

On the other hand, the law of incompleteness has a cheerful nip that is frequently missed by rationalist antagonists, who murmur that the quantum perspective leads science to founder on the shoals of absurdity. If science were as omnicompetent in its tasks and as Olympian in its gaze as mechanist thought has alleged, then the search for new knowledge would be cut short very quickly. Laplace and his imitators were persuaded that if science could stipulate the "initial conditions" of any physical system, it could thereby predict the future behavior and states of the system. In this attitude we can decipher the psychology of the mechanist. Any mechanist is confident he can predict what his invention will precisely do. Mechanistic science has been under the illusion that it contrived the laws of nature. But the machine can only produce what it is set up to do. It cannot acquire new knowledge.

This restriction is also imposed upon even complicated computers, which in accordance with what is known as Church's thesis must carry out their operations within a self-consistent axiomatic system (i.e., a "program"). They can interpret and validate *data* according to their own register of symbols. They can even modify the register if the "feedback" of data uncovers inconsistencies to the degree that such computers can be called "self-programming," which has been prematurely heralded by artificial intelligence enthusiasts as evidence of the possibility of authentic "thinking machines." Even a turkey may adjust its own "bioprogram," its battery of instinctual responses, to significant new stimuli, such as perhaps when a hound is trained to guard fowl rather than to savage them. The law of incompleteness signals that the universe, including that strange quirk of human self-awareness, is geared up not just for the production of data, but for the increase of information. Data and information are generally confused in the public mentality. Data is what can be generated from a closed system, which is what all self-referring, axiomatic ensembles happen to be. Information arises from an ongoing intercourse between the definite and the ambiguous, the theorem and its exception. And the new quantum science, as opposed to its mechanistic elder brother, is always in quest of novel settings for generating information. Like the Navajo weavers who never joined the first and last stitches of their prodigious tapestries, leaving the pattern open-ended because of their "superstition" it would be an affront to the universe, the quantum theorist is unwilling to finalize either his presuppositions or his findings out of respect for the "uncertainty relations" that entwine and "conjugate" every variable.

The centrality of the idea of information to the quantum world has been sketched out by the German physicist Friedrich von Weizsaecker. Von Weizsaecker has propounded his "postulate of expansion" according to which "the universe can be described as consisting of ultimate objects whose number increases in time."[7] A similar these is found in Whitehead. But Von Weizsaecker employs such a cosmology to accent the significance of information. Information is a relationship between material events in space and time. And the observed expansion of space necessitates the postulate of heightened information. If the universe is the totality of knowable forms, it must at any given time be finite. But the universe can acquire an additional finite amount of information in a finite time interval. Invoking the objectification of semantics, I interpret this growth in the amount of knowable form as the expansion of the universe. The growth of space, in this sense, *is* the openness of the future.[8] The growth of information, made possible through quantum indeterminacy, rubs against the materialist credo, whereby the laws of physical action are seen to be intrinsic to nature and the properties of any system can be derived "axiomatically" from these laws. As von Weizsaecker points out, for the materialist the prospect of matter becoming "conscious" is superfluous, inasmuch as all "information" is already programmed into physical laws. "In our view, however," according to von Weizaecker, matter is nothing but the possibility of the empirical decision of alternatives."[9] These alternatives, or indeterminate possibilities, constitute the array of universal information structures, only a cross-section of which is realized in the material realm. The requirement of a decision among alternatives to generate information "presupposes a subject who decides." Metaphysically speaking, "God is not the totality of forms, but their ground."[10]

A more colloquial rendering of the preceding statement is to say that God is the ground of all information. But let us be more incisive about what we have in mind when we talk about *information*. The word "information" is one of the most promiscuously used and habitually abused expressions in current scientific discourse. Sociologists chatter about the advent of the "information society." Librarians, who are routinely trained in graduate school to handle computers, have been renamed "information managers." Business economists converse about the dependence of corporate management on good "information flow." It is evident in all these instances that the edge is blurred between data and information. The concept of information,

---

[7] Friedrich von Weizsaecker, *The Unity of Nature*, trans. Francis Zucker (New York: Farrar, Strauss, Giroux, 1980), p. 219.

[8] von Weizsaecker, p. 293.

[9] von Weizsaecker, p. 293.

[10] von Weizsaecker, p. 294.

which has its genesis in the late nineteenth century physics, implies something more consequential to the universe than office memoranda and bibliographic citations. Technologically stored and processed "information" (i.e. data) can be characterized as complex codings of a constant energy pattern or "signal" through a series of binary modulations. "Modulation" means that the wave frequency is disrupted by interference from another signal or by variable switching on and off of the basic one. This variable switching yields the "message." One of the most simple examples is the telegraphic key, which whenever it is depressed breaks an electric connection and causes an uneven oscillation of the voltage potential in the line which can be translated back into letters by the receiver through the Morse code. Computers work the same way, except that they have innumerable "keys" and switches working in elaborate sequences. Each computer read-out is composed of myriad "yes-no" decisions that modulate the basic frequency, which is the approximately 60 cycles per second of standard house current. The coding of all binary decision information, on the other hand, is inherently linear. Just as a telegraph message can be analyzed into a line of dots and dashes, so the computerized "information" is broken up into hundreds and thousands of "bits" encoded into silicon microchips. When a computer "remembers" it simply reactivates the digitally stored message by playing back the originally modulated 60 cycle signal. Since electronic waves move close to the speed of light, the computer can solve logical and mathematical puzzles at an astounding rate.

But note that the computer has to perform each step in the operation *seriatim*. It would be as though each time we added $2 + 2$, we had to do the following in succession: "$0 + 1 = 1$, $1 + 1 = 2$, $2 + 1 = 3$, $3 + 1 = 4$, $(1 + 1) + (1 + 1) = 2 + 2$, $(1 + 1 + 1) + 1 = 2 + 2$, $3 + 1 = 2 + 2$, $2 + 2 = 4$. In principle, the computer "deduces" its answer by switching on all the implication of the axiomatic system for which it was programmed in a linear mode. The above procedure for axiomatic inference looks cumbersome on paper, but so do most computer programs. The computer is a speed reader, but it must still scan in a linear trajectory symbol by symbol. The human speed reader, however, does not have to pursue each letter and word in discursive fashion. He *sees* simultaneously packets of information as word figures, often on more than one line, according to the same process whereby we know straightway that $2 + 2 = 4$. In actuality, it is data or so-called "information bits" that flow. Information is the form the flux takes.

The confusion of information with data stems from certain muddled philosophical notions affiliated with the mathematical nomenlature of classical thermodynamics. Classical thermodynamics represented the effort to apply the Newtonian mechanics of motion to the phenomenon of heat energy. Heat energy is a function of the random movement of molecules. The famous "third law" of thermodynamics correlates inversely the availability of free energy for molecular motion with randomness on the level of *statistical probability*. A highly probable state of molecular system, i.e., on which is randomly distributed, has less free energy and tends toward maximum *entropy*. Entropy, which has become something of a chic philosophical idea for many today and a sociological rule for some misguided authors who barely apprehend its intricacy,[11] is really little more than a mathematical function that makes sense only in terms of statistical mechanics. Because entropy came to signify algebraically the quantity of "bound" energy in a closed, thermodynamic system, its obverse value referred to free energy or "information." In so-called "information theory," the fulcrum for computer mathematics built out of the linear equations of classical thermodynamics, every bit can be interpreted as a source of free variation. But information also depends on the promulgation of form or structure. As Rudolf Arnheim has made us aware, the linear paradigm of information mixes up the concept of "order" with randomization or entropy. Information can, therefore, be construed as a kind of disorder.

Yet genuine "information", in the sense of Weizsaecker's notion of what can perennially sire more information, betokens a dynamic equilibrium between convergent forces. Arnheim cites a classical experiment by Joseph Thomson. In Thomson's experiment magnetic needles of opposite polarity were inserted in corks and floated in water. Under normal circumstances of the magnets would repel and move away from each other at the specific angle of declination. However, when a large magnet was suspended at right angles to the plane of repulsion the needles all arranged themselves into a geometric picture. "Such demonstrations," Arnheim says, "show that orderly form will come about as the visible result of physical forces establishing, under field conditions, the most balanced configurations attainable."[12] Crystals and living organisms betray this tendency toward the reversal of entropy through intricate *structuration*.

Such structuration actually keeps the ambient energy unbound by preventing its dispersion willy-nilly. An example is quartz crystal, used in a passel of technological devices from digital watches to diodes. Electromagnetic energy can be both regulated and demodulated by the structural properties of the quartz, thus freeing it for various communication purposes and the transmission of "information" in the more familiar meaning of the word. The creation of complex ordering systems, such as human beings, is not contingent on the attainment of equilibrium, as is the case in classical thermodynamics, but on what Nobel prize-winning chemist Ilya Prigogine calls "dissipative structures." Such structures presuppose *less than* maximum randomization, the manageable tension, and controllable chaos. The study of dissipative structures marries thermodynamics in a nonmechanistic

---

[11] The most egregious example is the one-time bestseller by Jeremy Rifkin, *Entropy* (New York: Bantam Books, 1980).

[12] Rudolf Arnheim, *Entropy and Art* (Berkeley, CA: University of California Press, 1971), p. 6.

fashion to biology and cognitive psychology. It undergirds a science of open, *self-maintaining* feedback loops of computer theory) which Prigogine describes as the "physics of becoming."[13] Mechanistic physics has glorified in the "orderly" character of bound fields of energy where all phenomena can be calibrated with certainty, all motions commandeered, and all future states forecast. The end point of a mechanistic universe is cosmic entropy. The new physics stresses an inexhaustible reserve of free energy and increasing *negentropy* via the growth of structured information. The more structure, the more Weizsaeckerian "alternatives" we have in navigation a path through time and space. Information does not mean the lowest common denominator among quantum potentials. Information implies the manifestation of what is most improbable. Similarly, life and consciousness are the realization of increasingly improbable structures. A universe of maximal information, as opposed to one destined for an entropic collapse, demands Goedelian undecidaability. Goedel's God could never be a computer. The quantum revolution has delivered to us an incipient world model in which we are always privileged to perceive things differently from the norm. The "common sense" of the quantum era is a healthy suspicion toward everyday sensibility. That also holds good for our science which can no longer be considered, as the Victorian doyen Thomas Huxley put it, "trained and organized common sense." The common sense of the new science is an uncommon delight in quantum surprises. To quote once more the ancient Greek sage Heraclitus: "unless one expects the unexpected he wil not find truth." Heraclitus' insights, like quantum theory itself, must remain forever "incomplete."

[13] Ilya Prigogine, *From Being to Becoming: Time and Complexity in the Physical Sciences* (San Francisco, CA: W. H. Freeman & Co., 1980), p. 71.

CHAPTER 5

FROM DISCONTINUITY TO COMMUNITY IN SCIENCE

"True science is complete vision."

—FRIEDRICH SCHLEIERMACHER

Quantum thinking can be distilled down to a poetic maxim: *the universe is constantly blinking, but with each blink it beholds a consistent tableau.* Another way of stating the case is to say that the fundamental discontinuity between events observed in microphysics is overridden, when we reach gargantuan proportions, but the interrelatedness of all momenta. The broken continuum of mass and energy spelled out through Planck's constant is complemented paradoxically by what is referred to in the trade as "quantum inseparabililty." Quantum inseparability—i.e., the postulate that there are no isolated "objects" in the universe because of the mutual embroidery of all occurences with each other—was first exhibited mathematically, as was quantum discontinuity. Bell's theorem has never enjoyed the status of an empirical discovery. Nor is it a license for wooly-minded mysticism, as some gurus have been prone to do. It is more a logical touchstone. Just as Goedel's proof laid bare the limits of systematic rationalism, Bell's theorem puts restrictions on all atomistic or "pluralistic" world schemas. On the one hand, there can be no guarantee of formal certainty, as Descartes hoped. On the other hand, the alternative is not some Dionysian celebration of chaos, and the surrender of science to nihilism. Quantum inseparability, or "quantum interconnectedness", as it is also called, is actually a *sub-quantum* effect. In other words, the quantization of the fields of action in the cosmos conjures up the mirage of multiplicity. The sub-quantal distribution of things, which might better be regarded as "qualitative," is responsible for their unity.

If it were not for quantum inseparability, that invisible sub-assembly of "matter," the universe would be bereft of intelligence. Intelligence involves the discrimination of complex patterns beneath the undulating and agitated surface of phenomena. Creative scientists have possessed this gift of what in the older Gestalt psychology was called *Praegnanz*—the ability to manifest immanent themes of figures out of a mash of sensations and impressions. Intelligence relies on a tract of interworking field relationships which are more than mere "data" or singularities of knowledge. If we return to our

"connect the dots" analogy, we can see that intelligence, or the facility for
gaining structural information, is enhanced by the contemplation of *images*.
The image is more "concrete" than the abstract idea, insofar as it displays
subtle and minutely coherent features that cannot be captured in any set of
mathematical equations. "Indeterminacy," as quantum physics has defined
the issue, is relative to the act of measurement. Measurement itself is
accomplished by squeezing an infinitely maleable range of experience into
the Procrustean bed of quantifiable procedures. "Quantification," in which
orthodox science glories and which the artist or the humanist eschews,
means that we steer our attention to discrete quanta while ignoring their
interconnectedness. It is a case of concentrating on the dots, yet overlooking
the lines that couple them together. At the same time, following the dots is
necessary if the "image" is to form. Quantifying our experience is required to
give it some kind of stability, without which we would all be daft. Any image
may be etched upon a blank sheet of paper. The insertion of the dots
minimizes the possibility of counterfeits.

We must take another careful look at the nature of the enigmatic "quantum." The *quantization* of energy was a property detected around the turn of
the century in the endeavor to measure radiation instrumentally. The energy
seemed to come forth in "packages," or under certain circumstances, in
timed pulsations. Quantum radiation was first scrutinized in the form of
high-energy light corpuscles or "photons." By generalizing from the so-
called "photo-voltaic" effect in which a high-intensity beam will knock electrons out of their atomic orbits and produce a current, Einstein drew the
conclusion that light was best characterized as a particle. The word "particle"
implies "part" or "division" and thus stands in contrast to quantum interconnectedness. At the same time under conditions of diffraction, light also
appeared to be propagated in a wave-like stream. Thus arose the famous
"wave-particle" duality according to which electromagnetic energy could be
envisaged in either mode. Niels Bohr and some of his colleagues sought to
surmount this paradox by tendering the "complementarity thesis." According to the complementarity thesis, electromagnetic emanations are simultaneously waves and particles. Such a verdict, known also as the
"Copenhagen Interpretation" of quantum mechanics, may have reconciled
the discrepant results of physical experiement; but it has never gratified
professional philosophers. Investigation of the different ends of the electromagnetic spectrum have suggested that complementarity only works for
the middle bands. For example, extremely high energy gamma rays show
only negligible wave behavior. Very low energy magnetic phenomena (so
called "extra low frequency" or ELF waves used for sophisticated submarine
communication) display few particle-like properties. Furthermore, quantization is more meaningful, though in theory it applies all the way across, the
further we ascend the high frequency ladder.

Planck's formula says that the greater the wave frequency, the more energy it has. The converse is also true. On an oscilloscope, which presents a graphic counterpart for electomagnetic fluctuations, a very low frequency wave will look virtually like a straight line. The peaks and troughs of the wave are barely noticeable. The peaks of the wave correspond roughly to the bundles of energy identified as corpuscles or "little bodies" in early quantum theory. The troughs denote the gap between the bundles or pulsations. After Louis Broglie convinced his colleagues fifty years ago that electrons are not just particles in the conventional connotation, but are also specimens of what he dubbed "matter waves," a puzzle arose as to what the waves themselves constituted. Max Born, who garnered the Nobel Prize for his research in quantum mechanics, asserted that electron oscillations were "probability waves," mathematical portrayals of the chance of finding the minuscule particles in a particular position at a given time. The same extrapolation would compass, too, the case of light waves. The higher energy of the wave, the greater the frequency of its statistical "distributuon" at a given quantum level, and the more the wave field can be said to be quantized, and by the same token the more it can be "measured" in the normal understanding of the word. Very low frequency waves, especially those outside the range of our senses, do not lend themselves so easily to quantization. The reason is patent. Both their energy and their probability density are small. Like the rotation of the earth, they are not evident to our perception, but their presence is appreciable nonetheless. It should also be recalled that the "uncertainty" of observation for a subatomic particle posited by Heisenberg had to do with sense observation. If our eyes were able to "see" at a much lower frequency than we do (e.g., with microwave sensors), we might not incur Heisenberg's problem.

In short, quantum interconnectedness may be the outgrowth of low frequency wave interactions far below the sensory as well as the instrumental threshold. Take the example of swells on the ocean. Because of our size and sweep of vision as human beings, we can glimpse both the larger, rolling wave motions and the diminutive splashes, wrinkles, and disturbances that constitute the surface flux. A tiny sea horse riding the billows, however, would only discern the surface flux—the minute bursts and blimps that manifest in the sea horse's immediate surroundings—would come across to him as discontinuous "quanta," and he would most likely construe the surging of the sea as a featureless vacuum. But a subquantal observer would know better. He would see the interconnectedness of all wave perturbations, large and small. And he would see the pattern of motion which the seahorse in his preoccupation with what was close at hand would leave out of account.

A significant philosophical overview of quantum interconnectedness has been supplied by the British theoretical physicist David Bohm. Bohm distinguishes between the "implicate" and the "explicate" orders. The explicate order consists in that domain of information which can be processed by the senses, conceptualized, and rendered with mathematical exactness. Regular science takes this region of explicate relationships as the whole of reality. But what it forgets is that it has simply objectified its own constructs. The "objects" which both science and sense awareness encounter in the external world are actually representations of the intellect. These representations, which make up the furniture of the explicate universe, however, have their origin, for Bohm, in a vast, multi-dimensional expanse, whereby "a *total order* is contained in some implicit sense, in each region of space and time."[1] This total order is like an enormous switchboard of information—some might call it the cosmic mind itself—where all thoughts or messages can be relayed instantaneously. But even the idea of "instantaneity" becomes strained, inasmuch within the implicate order our everyday three-dimensional apprehension of time and space becomes impertinent. The alleged "wave-particle duality" reflects mainly the different modalities of consciousness and experiment for reckoning countless ripples on the void, or what we might term "wrinkles" in the implicate order. When the wrinkles are spread out in space, there is a wave. When they are spread out in time, we have a particle. And all the ripples or wrinkles are but vibrations of a single underlying stuff. This distinction becomes apparent in a mathematical as well as a metaphysical vein. If we enlist what are called "Fourier transformations," we find that a dimensionless point can be expanded to produce a sine wave of infinite frequencies occupying all of space and time. Richard Feynman, inventor of the "Feynman diagrams" for mapping the trajectories in space-time of sub-moleculat events, once announced the "crazy" conjecture that every electron he saw in his cloud chamber might actually be an outcropping of the same electron. This sentiment in the past few years has been adopted in the speculative theory of "strings."

Feynman's crazy notion is, of course, not that crazy after all. Bohm declares: "what is implied by this proposal (of the implicate order) is that what we call empty space contains an immense background of energy, and that matter as we know it is a small, 'quantized' wavelike excitation on tip of this background . . ."[2] The quantization of the space background—the complete wave motion—occurs because of its intersection with the time dimension. We should recall Planck's discovery was that energy "manifests" or is quantized according to frequency; and frequency expresses the distribution of energy in time. The interconnectedness of quanta may be regarded as the total wave field of the universe, and the quanta themselves might possibly be identified anew as the minuscule "perforations" of the time membrane by the space-like wave form. Feynman's monolithic electron may in itself be an appendage of what we might jocularly call the "total particle" which in itself belongs within the frequency region of the absolute. The absolute breathes,

---

[1] David Bohm, *Wholeness and the Implicate Order* (London: Routledge & Kegan Paul, 1980), p. 149.
[2] Bohm, p. 191.

shudders, gyres, and reshapes itself in a multitude of quivering patterns and forms. The potentiality of the wave is transformed into the actuality of the material "body", which has a certain career in time and then dissipates. In short, it returns to what Heisenberg referred to as the universe of *potentia*, the cosmic wave, which is Bohm's implicate order. This constant and highly intricate process in which objects emerge from their implicit matrix and return Bohm calls the "holomovement." It is the movement of the whole within and out of itself along the crease of time. Bohm draws a parallel with the California live oak tree which is green all year round. He says: ". . .the live oak tree is an example of some-thing which in a gross observation always looks very nearly the same, and yet the dying and being regenerated are going on constantly side by side. And interpenetrating the leaves which are dying are leaves which are being regenerated."[3] The leaves are the quanta; the tree is the universe *tout ensemble*. In a sense every time the universe becomes quantized it winks, and each wink is a moment of matter in time.

Although the concept of quantum interconnectedness smacks of old-style, idealistic metaphysics, it springs in truth from the sorts of rigorous mathematical deductions that occupied quantum mechanics at the outset. It is true that many physicists even today balk at the kind of cosmological reverie which has conferred on Bohm his special reputation. Their objection is that quantum theory amounts to nothing more than an attempt to explain instrumental readings. Hence, they would deny any metaphysical overtones above and beyond what the dials on their machines say. Such a position is in itself "metaphysical." It accords the status of supreme reality to the act of measurement. The philosophical tradition that gave rise to this prejudice is known as "positivism." Positivism has been a highly influential ideology in the late modern period, which has made a holy grail of quantitative abstractions. But quantum physics was spawned, as we have seen, out of the attempt to make meaningful a clutch of experimental peculiarities, together with the failure to find strategies for strict quantification of the rowdy goings-on beneath the beach blanket of the "material." Therefore, it has been metaphysical in its ramifications from day one. Many of the same positivist critics have also been alarmed at the talk of "strangeness" and "paradox" surrounding the physicists' reporting of quantum effects. But those labels accurately designate what is happening in a roundly "experimental" setting. Metaphysical extravagances are at least consistent. The fundamental givens of quantum operations are *not*.

What exactly were these experimental serenipities and oddities that demand a refurbishing of the evidence? There are seemingly exhaustless subtleties to the problems which have been ritually reviewed in both scien-

---

[3] Renee Weber, "The Enfolding-Unfolding Universe: A Conversation with David Bohm," in Ken Wilber (ed.), *The Holo-Graphic Paradigm and Other Paradoxes* (Boulder, Co: Shambala, 1982), p. 81.

tific and philosophical literature. But the essential issue is not so complicated. The issue can be posed as follows: in what degree can the statistical
probabilities which quantum mechanics substituted for outright prediction
be accepted as representations of "real" nature? The dilemma was exacer-
bated by the confusion among philosophers of science interested in quantum
theory over such probabilistic statements. The logical formality of mathematics, especially because of the sway of Bertrand Russell, was taken as
equivalent to the cipher of knowledge about, as Ludwig Wittgenstein had
put it, "all that is the case." But could potential, rather than realized, states
of a quantum system (what are technically called "eigenstates") be conceded
as real, even if they might be depicted by the extremely versatile probability
calculus and matrix algebra refined by the turn of the century? Potential
states were as real to the quantum mechanical investigator as jiggling molecules were to the physical chemist.

Erwin Schroedinger touched off a minor earthquake in the early phases
of quantum mechanics by writing a set of equations which incorporated
potential states. The denotation for the general wave field in which the sum
of potential quantum states is contained Schroedinger gave as the Greek
letter or "psi." Psi-states could be assigned a probability value as an index of
their basic *tendency to be*. These varying probabilities fall within the general
wave equation. The actual, as opposed to the potential, state of a system
comes from the precipitation of certain probabilities. In quantum mechanics
a particle comprises "wave packet" of potentialities that have "collapsed" into
a definite configuaration. The collapse of the wave packet is juxtaposed with
the event of observation, where a discrete but probable constellation now
conforms to the conditions of the observer and his apparatus. Another
figurative way of characterizing what occurs is to say that the measurement
serves to carve out and serve up a "piece of the psi-function. The part that
has been excised happens to coincide with what we glibly and parochially
vaunt as "reality."

Schroedinger drove this point home with what has come to be known as
his "cat paradox." The cat paradox is frequently cited nowadays as a teaser in
introducing new readers to quantum theory. But we shall reiterate it nonetheless. Suppose, Schroedinger argued, you place a cat in a hermetically
sealed box to which is attached a device that releases a lethal dose of cyanide
to the hapless beast. The release of the cyanide is triggered by the decay of a
radioactive particle which has, say, a half-life of ten minutes. After ten
minutes you are ready to open the box. Is the cat dead or alive? There is a
fifty-fifty chance that either result has ensued. So probability computations
cannot lighten the difficulty. Schroedinger's answer: it makes no sense to
speak of the animal as dead or alive until you *open the box*, or until you
manifest one or two equivalent eigenstates through observation. If opening
the door discloses that the cat is dead, then the wave function (or "state
vector" as it is alternately named) has collapsed upon that specific poten-

tiality. In the case of equal compossibilities, there are absolutely no grounds for making accurate predictions by appeal to independent variables. Hence the supposition that the dead cat is somehow stamped within the texture of reality becomes ludicrous.

An even more provocative sidetrack to Schroedinger's thought experiment was his suggestion that if the cat is found to be dead, it remains yet alive within the other half of the wave function! If the wave function is abridged upon observation, then the portion that has not "collapsed" or been "reduced" must still somehow continue, like the tail of a flatworm that has been sliced at midriff. A more relativistic position would be that the dead cat "section" of the psi-wave, in which contradictory eigenstates can coexist, has merely been "selected out" by the universal tuner that is consciousness and the live cat component suppressed.

The suggestion of a fissioned psi-wave as the explanation for the transition from potential to actual was behind what might be hallowed as the original metaphysical interpretation of quantum mechanics. Such an interpretation is the now celebrated "many worlds hypothesis" of theoretical physicist Hugh Everett. According to Everett, whenever the cortege of events encounters a set of compossibles, consciousness makes a "choice" and the universe forks. For every time-bound occasion there exist a number of alternative worlds that are cognate with or exist parallel to each other and can be brought into being, depending on the disposition and capacity of the observer! Everett enunciates this proposition in rather pedantic language. "To any arbitrary choice of state for one subsystem, which will correspond a *relative* state for the other subsystem, which will generally be dependent on the choice of state for the first subsystem, so that the state of one subsystem is not independent, but correlated to the state of the remaining subsystem."[4] The correlation of "subsystems" to which Everett refers is, of course, that of the conjugate variables, the alternate eigenstates. The universal wave function seems to act like a mirror in which we are looking at a scene along with its reflection, but at the same time we cannot easily distinguish between which one is "real" and which one virtual. Perhaps it does not matter! Sometimes we "enter" into the world on the other side; sometimes we stay where we are.

Bernard d'Espagnat has described how various experiments involving the spin of paired protons underscores this correlation of worlds.[5] In a singular instance of observation the spin of the one proton will always be opposite to that of the other. This division may be a primitive instance of the

[4] Hugh Everett, "The Theory of the Universal Wave Function," in Bryce Dewitt (ed.), *The Many-Worlds Interpretation of Quantum Mechanics* (Princeton, NJ: Princeton University Press, 1973), p. 10.

[5] Bernard d'Espagant, "The Quantum Theory and Reality," *Scientific American* 241 (1979):158–81.

polarization of reality due to consciousness or observation. But there are further consequences. The pairing of opposed spins among protons and electrons may very well confirm the interconnectedness of quanta beneath the skin of our individuated experiences. That is d'Espagnat's conclusion. It makes no sense to talk about a causal relationship between the disparate spin moments. They are our famed conjugate variables. And they are "conjugate" if we understand the basic force of the word. "Conjugation" means that what is essentially unitary can be divided without losing its wholeness. Conjugation of quantum observables constitutes the great "yin and yang" of the universe. The universal wave function may be imagined as like a huge swatch of sheet metal. When furrowed in one spot, it pushes up in an adjoining area. All knowledge and each scientific discovery is a solemn sacrifice of what might otherwise be. But this sacrifice merely involves a split between what we can and cannot see. The roads taken and not taken are yet the same thoroughfare.

In the same breath we should cast a chary eye at the enthusiasm for *quantum mechanical magic* in which subjective consciousness somehow "causes" the collapse of the wave function. Such a view has had a heady impact upon the campaign to wed the "new physics" to California-bred pop mysticism and parapsychological experimentation. It is ingredient in the novels of neo-occultist philosophy of the widely read author Robert Anton Wilson.[6] It is also the guiding wisdom in Fred Alan Wolf's award-winning book *Taking the Quantum Leap: The New Physics for Non-Scientists*. Wolf's contention is that Everett's "many worlds" through which parade numerous and lush quantum wave functions are comparable to booths in a cosmic bazaar within which we can opt for our own "slice" of reality. The decision among quantum options is as free and easy as buying a new skirt in a boutique. The trick is simply right belief and resolve. Wolf hands us a handsomely engraved invitation to sporting among "branches" of the all-inclusive quantum wave function ("qwiff"). "So what can you do? Anything you want to. You are doing it. To get any branch of the multiple—branching, universal qwiff is simple. Just become aware of what you want to do. From any branch there is a pathway leading to any other branch . . . keep making the impossible possible. Keep choosing which branch you wish to sample life on."[7] The flavor, of course, is distinctly that of the New Age narcisissm in which values and even worlds are spun out of the overrich imagination of the middle class knight errant. The "mystery and miracle" interpretation of quantum mechanics happens to be a caricature. Like all caricatures, it has a foothold in factuality. The play among potential worlds in the protean profusion of states prior to measurement does suggest an opportunity for creative

---

[6] See *inter alia* Robert Anton Wilson, *Cosmic Trigger* (Berkeley, CA: And/Or Press, 1977).
[7] Fred A. Wolf, *Taking the Quantum Leap: The New Physics for Non-Scientists* (New York: Harper & Row, 1981), p. 227.

manipulation on the part of the observer. It therefore has a mythic appeal that can be obviously pushed too far by the perennial partisans in American society of "mind over matter." Moreover, it is a somewhat healthy antidote to the dogmas of mechanism.

Nonetheless, such a representation of the quantum revolution to an inquisitive populace is misleading, if not noxious. And it has the unfortunate consequence of making quantum theory seem like the fifth column of pseudo-science. It is certainly an affront to the legacy of Bohr. As Max Jammer, historian of quantum mechanics has remarked: "Theoretical physicists, however revolutionary in their views professed *ex cathedra*, were brought up and live in a classical world."[8] Bohr himself flaunted his "correspondence principle" according to which all quantum mechanical inferences must have a counterpart within the classical syntax. The correspondence principle, fortunately or unfortunately, cannot be extended to cover every base. Goedel's limitations apply even to the translation of one scientific language into another. But there is a continuity between the old and the new physics which is cavalierly scanted by certain champions of "permanent revolution" in culture, which happens to include science.

If the phenomena of the universe are woven together in a filigree of "inseparability" in a potential or subquantal matter, it is rather inconsistent to make the solitary observer or dreamer a wizard in the mastery of probabilities. Such a wizard turns out to be much like the Wizard of Oz— champion of bluff, but a tyro when it comes to the real transformation of systems. The collapse of quantum wave functions (Wolf calls them "popping qwiffs") is due as much to certain kinds of intelligent decisions within Bohm's "implicate order." It is only a vanity of our contemporary psycho-culture that we shrink consciousness down to propensities of the lone subject. After Einstein physics sloughed off the mechanistic trifle that matter is a lattice of point-masses. Now that quantum theory has acquired a distinctive "idealist" bent, it cannot sumble into the same *punctiform fallacy* in its understanding of the interworkings of mind and nature. Bohm's implicate order becomes explicate *not* because one among a million different point-consciousnesses wants to live in world A rather than world B. Einstein thought God was too wise to spend eternity playing dice. He had to plan things as well. Bohm, although he never has succeeded in answering the "why" of what is implicit in the greater cosmos, tells us that it is the result of "an intelligence beyond any of the energies that could be defined in thought" which "directly transforms matter."[9] Subjects or point-consciousnesses are like the tiny filings in the force lines of a magnet. By themselves they move capriciously and become distorted in their configurations. The wider intelligence of the

[8] Max Jammer, *The Philosophy of Quantum Mechanics* (New York: John Wiley Sons, 1974), p. 253.
[9] "The Enfolding-Unfolding Universe," p. 67.

implicate order attracts them into a formative field whereby they take on the particular qualities they display. The bedevilling "randomness" of quantum events may not be so random after all. The usual conception of "random" is indistinguishable from "arbitrary." And science, even when it supplants propositions about natural "law" with statistical congregates of data, stands aghast at any suggestion it must leave certain subject matter completely up for grabs. The randomness apparent in the behavior of quanta many betray, in point of fact, a transcendent intelligence that refuses to kowtow to any scientific algorithm—Newtonian, Einsteinian, or Heisenbergian. Randomness is the wraith of our own ignorance; it may on the contrary be nothing less, as the Soviet physicist V. V. Nalimov has provocatively proposed, than a rune for "maximum complexity."[10] If any art connoiseur with classicist tastes gazes at a Gothic rose window he may be appalled at the foliation of "random" images. The Romantic mind will appreciate the pattern as some kind of "divine" emanation. Quantum physics has little to do with mysticism per se, but it may indeed be our first Gothic science.

The universal wave function is thus not divisible into eigenstates of high and low potentiality which can be snatched willy-nilly from the probability matrix like candy at a school carnival. The resolution of the problem of what in the wave field gets quantized and what has to stay warming the bench is decided not by the "players" (i.e., point-consciousnesses of individual entities), but by the "coach," the cosmic supermind. The players, of course, have "free will" in that they can play poorly or even defy the coach's authority. But the coach will end up shuffling the roster and even the personnel to attain the most co-ordinated and optimal performance. The wave function has a profound and hidden intelligence. Quantum interconnectedness betokens a veritable community of possibility; but it also indicates an unfathomed pool of intelligence. We recall Einstein's oft-quoted comment that "God may be subtle, but he is not malicious." His subtilty is sufficient to make it look as if he is winsomely playing draughts when in fact he is redesigning the universe. Einstein would not have been so uneasy with quantum theory if he had discerned how subtle *Herr Gott*, as he called him, just might be.

This solution to many quantum mechanical muddles is, therefore, what we might term the *cosmic supervisor*. Admittedly, it smacks very strongly of the old-fashioned theism that was tucked away in a dusty cupboard a hundred years ago or so; but it may be the only way for the fly of theoretical consistency to escape from the quantum mechanical flybottle. The difference between such a quantum *metaphysics* and the more rancid specimens of religious orthodoxy resides in the fact that our cosmic supervisor is not a pseudo-material agent, as He was for Newton, but pure intelligence. The quantum divinity prefers chess to craps. The postulate of the cosmic super-

---

[10]V. V. Nalimov, *Faces of Science* (Philadelphia: ISI Press, 1981), p. 180.

visor, first of all, eliminates the temptation to view the quantum universe as
one of anarchic indeterminacy. It was that very temptation which made
Einstein uncomfortable with the quantum tableau. Anarchic indeterminacy,
however, logically ensues if we attempt to construct a world model from our
instrumental readings and our computational recipes alone. The paragon of
anarchic indeterminacy is the so-called "von Neumann chain," another
thought experiment like Schroedinger's cat which has forced physicists to
meditate on first philosophy. It is named after John von Neumann, a physicist, who has also had a major influence on the theorists of artificial intelligence.[11]

Von Neumann noted the problem of any future philosophy of quantum
mechanics is bound up with the muddle of measurement. It was the earliest
experiment in subatomic research which generated the bewilderment over
the status of "observation," since heretofore there had been little doubt in
science that the "facts" of measurement revealed nature's unyielding laws.
But such facts, especially when it came to Lilliputian masses and subtle
energies, turned out to be a bit spurious. The state of measurement was seen
to be the coagulation of many different wave forms in a "packet" or grouping.
Prior to measurement we have a "superposition" of many vectors, each
indicating the phenomenon under observation and having one in a medley of
possible values. According to von Neumann, these vactors can be said to
collapse into a measurement (sometimes called "degenerate") state only if we
have a clear idea who or what is doing the measurement. Suppose we have an
electron observation contrivance specially assembled for such a feat. Unless
our own minds are co-extensive with the contrivance, which they are not, we
are compelled to conclude that the measuring apparatus itself exists in a
hyppothetical infinity of eigenstates, and hence its state vector must also be
collapsed, and so on. The von Neumann chain is the quantum mechanical
analogue to Zeno's paradox. Zeno was the Greek philosopher who "proved"
that Achilles, though swifter, could never catch up with the tortoise who was
in the lead of a race, because he would have to traverse infinitely small
increments of distance which could not be accomplished in a finite amount of
time.

From a logical point of view Zeno's paradox tells us we can never get
anywhere, which is empirically preposterous. Similarly, from the standpoint
of quantum mechanical formalism we can never truly measure a system,
which again is silly. The object lesson is once more the Goedelian incommensurability between representation and experience. The corollary is that we
must not objectify, or construct a cosmology, out of the peculiarities of
perception. *The finite cannot contain the infinite.* All attempts to do so lead
to von Neumann chains and Everett's multiplication of copy-cat worlds. As

---

[11] See John von Neumann, *Mathematical Foundations of Quantum Mechanics* (Princeton:
Princeton University Press, 1955).

Bryce Dewitt has remarked about such metaphysical junket, "here is schizo-phrenia with a vengeance."[12]

Observational subjectivism of the kind espoused by Wolf may, on the one hand, be lauded as proper, if not wholly agreeable, counterstroke to the menace of quantum madness. The other is, of course, a neo-Cartesian cybernetic formalism along the lines recommended by Douglas Hofstadter. Hofstadter insists that "non-quantum-mechanical computational models of mind and all that goes along with mind) are possible in principle."[13] Hofstadter's program is essentially deterministic. The collapse of the state vector stems not from any arbitrary intervention of "consciousness." Con-sciousness can be reduced to highly sophisticated and hierarchical webs of linear representations. Conscious choice itself Hofstadter describes as "a complicated internal configuration, established through a long history that encode tendencies toward certain future internal configuration and away from others."[14] Hofstadter draws a parallel with a windchime which seems to have a "will of its own." The illusion of will, Hofstadter charges, is the consequence of the intricate alternation and simultaneous rotations of the innumerable parts. But the wind is the prime mover all the same. In the case of mind the "wind" happens to be a program.

Both Wolf's and Hofstadter's defenses against the incipient insanity of a probabilistic universe are "neurotic" in an important sense. The neurotic is incapable of integrating into his world scheme the inscrutable, so he obliter-ates it with one full swing. The subjectivist says "I am the Creator myself." The cybernetic formalist pipes: "But your I is but an operator in a computer command system." So who writes the ultimate program? Perhaps our cosmic supervisor, whom we must always understand as a grand sort of metaphor, a heuristic notion in the Kantian sense. And who wants to argue that the structure of our own intelligence is any different from the programmer?

God is infinite intelligence. Human intelligence is potentially infinite. Computers are replicas of actual human intelligence. Therefore, like state vectors, they are finite. We lose the sense of the universe when we stuff the infinite into the finite. For the infinite is the universal community of quanta. If the mind is computer-like, it is cut off from the community. If the cybernetic reductionists were on the track with their world model, then an electron would have a higher I. Q. than a human being. Under certain conditions such as very cold temperatures an electron may "tunnel" out of its comfortable prison cell in local space-time and "pop" up somewhere else. The ultilization of electron-tunneling in solid state technology was a critical breakthrough in the field of microprocessing. In essence, an electron is smart

[12] Bryce Dewitt, "Quantum Mechanics and Reality," *Physics Today* (Sept. 1970): 33.
[13] Douglas R. Hofstadter, *The Mind's I: Fantasies and Reflections on Self and Soul* (New York: Basic Books, 1981), p. 43.
[14] Hofstadter, p. 198.

enough to know how to behave non-linearly, to represent itself in the idiom of quantum interconnectedness. It has a unique kind of "tunnel vision," which is actually a strand of Bohm's holomovement. Feynman's many faces of the monolithic electron can be reinterpreted as the ongoing manifestation of an infinite mind.

CHAPTER 6

THE OMNIJECTIVE UNIVERSE*

"Science is simply a magical set of rules and attitudes that works in
a certain limited context of experience."
—JACK SARFATTI

At this point, we shall advance three theses that should buffet the
lacquered pieties of post-enlightenment thought. First, our hallowed "experimental science" does not yield any foolproof method of verification; but,
as the Sarfatti quotation above indicates, amounts to a sophisticated king of
conjuration. Second, the much vaunted "empirical" bias of modern inquiry,
which assesses truth statements as to their agreement with sense data, and
which brushes aside as nonsense all modes of discourse pertaining to the
transcendent dimension of knowledge and experience, proves on meticulous
inspection to be the opposite of what it appears, viz., a thoroughly "rational"
and all-encompassing procedure. Instead it can be exposed as the great
superstition of our post-theological generation. Third, the cherished ideal of
"objectivity," to which all orders in the broad clerisy of secular learning
intone their vows of allegiance, turns out to be nought but perspectival
warping of a broader focus which the physicist John Wheeler has dubbed
"observership." The same applies to what we might brand the "myth" of
subjectivity.

The foregoing remarks, together with their tacit challenge to the magisterium of present day philosophy and scientism, are not the froth of
Romantic sentimentality. On the contrary, they are variations on some of the
more fundamental propositions that can be articulated within the current
domain of theoretical physics. Many of the familiar epistemological questions
that have remained knotted and unresolved in modern philosophy of science
(e.g., the persistent conundrum concerning the relation of hypothesers to
evidentiary statements) must slip away with the introduction of a new cosmological overview. Logic, semantics, and criteriology—the central philosophical obsessions of our day—are, like cosmology itself, outcroppings of
the same "paradigm." Yet the word "paradigm," which Thomas Kuhn in-

*An earlier version of this chapter appeared in *Contemporary Philosophy* 8 (Fall 1981): 2–5.
Reprinted with permission.

tended only to designate the gist of scientific deliberations, perhaps falls short in conveying the scope of the greater intellectual reversals and changeovers that affect not only routine fact-gathering, but the more global formal, and cultural styles of reflection. Scientific paradigms are core components of what Gerald Holton has denoted as "themata", Michel Foucault as the variety of "episteme", Nelson Goodman simply as "worlds." Goodman *inter alia* has shown us that even cosmology, which we are apt to esteem as a sort of pristine and inviolable bastion of inquiry, is itself a project of a particular "world." As Goodman states, "this world . . . is the one most often taken real; for reality in a world, like realism is a picture, is largely a matter of habit."[1] Furthermore, it is the nature of a habit to be constricting and selective. Thus, within the perimeter of every "world" a discrete topological bias develops, whereby certain features are set in relief and others acquire a blurred focus, if they do not slip from sight altogether. For, in Goodman's words, "our capacity for overlooking is virtually unlimited."[2] Our unbounded myopia may be the leading clue to the discovery that the universe—in which are subsumed as well our historically configured "universes" of discourse—is itself without limitation. The axiom of illimitability constitutes one of the ontological cornerstones of quantum physics.

But the illimitable, or *infinite*, character of the cosmos does not amount to an empty set. For the illimitability of the universe, according to quantum physics, does not imply the indeterminacy of things so much as it connotes their inseparability. This assumption, i.e., the "quantum inseparability principle", bears a remarkable resemblance to Hegel's "good infinity," wherein the "concept" *(Begriff)* of an entity is established not as a cognitive isolate, but as a network of connections. Such relationships are not traced out between "knower" and "known," or between "subject" and "object," but between what David Bohm has labelled the "implicate" and "explicate" facets of the cosmic totality. Hence, it is one-sided and inappropriate to discern phenomena from either the "subjective" or the "objective" angle of vision. Instead we must see the universe as *omnijective*—a term coined by Michael Talbot.[3]

The notion of an "omnijective" universe, in which both things and events are infinitely and intimately interstitched with each other, has grown with the elaboration of quantum theory.[4] The Einstein-Podolsky-Rosen paper 1935 sought to prove that quantum theory was self-contradictory and there-

[1] Nelson Goodman, *Ways of Worldmaking* (Indianapolis, IN: Hackett, 1978), p. 20.

[2] Goodman, p. 14.

[3] See Michael Talbot, *Mysticism and the New Physics* (New York: Bantam Books, 1980).

[4] Another popular book on quantum physics, which elaborates many of the same themes— i.e., the isomorphism of the new cosmology of quantum interconnectedness and classical forms of mysticism—is Gary Zukav, *The Dancing Wu Li Masters* (New York: William Morrow, 1979). It should be noted, however, that the mystical interpretation of quantum mechanics is only an extreme variant on the holistic model, which depends on the inferences of Bell's theorem.

fore untenable. According to Einstein-Podolsky-Rosen, if quantum theory is correct, then all particles must be in instantaneous communication with each other, even if they are spread out over vast distances. This conclusion contradicted special relativity, which had by then achieved prestige in the scientific community, and which forbade both effects of "simultaneity" and the possibility of "superluminal" (i.e., faster than light) information transfer. In addition, it appeared that quantum mechanics could not pick up the gauntlet Einstein and his confreres had thrown down. Yet thirty years later the weight of plausibility began to swing in favor of the quantum approach, whereas it became clear that Einstein's reasonings were sound, but applicable only across a range of observations. Just as Einstein himself had proposed that the Newtonian laws of motion wre not invalid, but had to be circumscribed within the sphere of terrestrial velocities, so quantum theory has of late made it plain that special relativity makes sense only within the parameters of space-time. And, as the discovery of black holes and the postulate of time-warps intimates, space-time may not be the seamless garment physics has all along presumed. Space-time itself may very well be punctuated with lesions that have come to be described as "singularities" beyond whose "event horizons" all the recognizable laws of physics must vanish.

Regardless of what popular opinion holds, special relativity did not completely revamp Newtonian science. Einstein's cosmology was to Newton's as thirteenth century churches were to the earlier Romanesque basilicas. Ceilings were raised, the transept extended, and flying buttresses built on so as to make the modern cathedral of scientific intellect more monumental and lofty. Yet the same *ecclesia* with its rudimentary assumptions about reality were left intact. For instance, Einstein's lifelong discomfort with the logic of quantum thinking did not stem simply from his preference for invariances over probabilistic functions; it issued from his instinctive abhorrence of the idea that correlations between happenings in the universe might be acausal or "non-local" (as the physicists say), which was hinted, but never corroborated, by the pioneers of quantum mechanics through their own mathematical equations. Despite David Hume's attack in the eighteenth century on all realistic interpretations of causalistic doctrine, modern science had proceeded all along from the very premise, which it reckoned as a milestone of method, if not ontology. The stance of causalism was inextricably bound up with the priority awarded within the modern *Weltanschauung* to space and time, whether space and time were portrayed as "absolute" substrata of motion, as Newton imagined, or whether they could be adduced critically as *a priori* forms of intuitions in Kant's sense. Einstein, together with Minkowski, merely mapped afresh the "geometry" of space-time and, accordingly, revised the rules for plotting the trajectory of bodies and causal sequences throughout the manifold of physical changes.

Yet the insuperability of the space-time manifold was never brought into question. Causal linkages, or local conjunctions, were the only intelligible strands that could be examined by science. Furthermore, causalism presupposes the existence of independent and self-contained entities, or agents, which interact with lawlike consistency at calculable positions in the spacetime reference frame. Without the supposition of discrete divisions in the order of things (what has been tabbed "Einstein separability") causal junctures between phenomena would either make no sense, or they would be superfluous, so far as scientific hypotheses were involved. Hence, when confronted with the notorious wave-particle paradox of electromagnetic radiation, the followers of Einstein sought an explanation along the lines of corpuscular behavior. The quantum theorists, on the other hand, opted for the statistical projections of wave mechanics, and thus the photon, lacking any definite set of co-ordinates and undermining the preferred, "fundamentalist" (as Capra uses the expression) notion of material "things" in a spacetime matrix.

Einstein separability had the initial advantage over quantum inseparability (alternately referred to as "quantum interconnectedness"), not only because the latter was counterintuitive, but also because the former squared with the categories of the Western metaphysical tradition, not to mention everyday common sense. For a while many physicist hoped to heal the breach between the partisans of locality and champions of quantum inseparability in the same manner as the wave-particle duality had been "solved" with Bohr's precept of "complementarity." However, such an irenic agenda was disrupted by Bell's theorem. According to Bell's theorem, either the statistical basis of quantum mechanics or Einstein separability is wrong. Mathematically, the two cannot be reconciled. Since the advent of Bell's theorem, the mathematical extrapolations of quantum theory have gained confirmation. And the more esoteric elements of Bell's theorem itself are on the verge of vindication through experimental research. Moreover, the most startling conclusion to be drawn from Bell's theorem is that non-locality without qualification implies in which all parts are in integral correspondence with each other. All events in both space and time "touch" each other in a reciprocal manner.

In such a universe, which we have already described as "omnijective," there can be neither pure chance nor blind fate. Chance means that particles have no overall communication among themselves, except when they are contiguous to each other. The idea of fate rests on the assumption that the universe is a rigid hierarchy in which information is passed along in a single direction on narrow tracks through a closed "chain of command." Past influences the future, but not the future the past. Bell's theorem laid the groundwork for the validation of the omnijective world hypothesis, yet it could not in itself serve as a cosmological construct to account precisely for the reciprocity of information quanta among the different subregions of space-time.

Inasmuch as quantum physics, combining the subtilties of Bell's theorem, is still a fledgling as well as *avante-garde* itinerary for speculation, the specification of such a construct has consisted in only a few, tentative attempts. One of these efforts is both intriguing and "sensible" to the extent that it does not make more than a few robust leaps across the moat of scientific orthodoxy. The second is more venturesome, although it had already spawned a number of fruitful analogies in other provinces of research, while the first has not.

The first construct, or prototype, was inaugurated by John Wheeler. In his trailblazing book *Geometrodynamics* Wheeler set forth the radical view that space-time is not, as relativity theory maintained, a system of relationships between "objects" or events, but that object/events are themselves fluctuations in space-time. Furthermore, space-time has a dynamic and metamorphic character in keeping with what Wheeler terms the "principle of universal mutability." The principle of universal mutability is founded on the idea that space-time, or what Wheeler designates simply "space," is forever folding, undulating, and even fissuring at particular stress points, which we know as "black holes." Wheeler invents a colorful illustration, that of space as a kind of "sausage skin."

". . . space is like an empty sausage skin, which is "floppy" and deprived of all resistance to bending until it has been filled with sausage meat. The "sausage meat" is the zero-point energy of particles and fields.[5] A second metaphor of Wheeler is that of space as a "quantum foam," which is constantly surging and rolling like an ocean tempest; there constantly appear myriad, tiny "singularities" where space-time conditions are suspended. These minute perforation of the spatio-temporal membrane (Jack Sarfatti has called them "virtual black holes" do not merely reveal the void, but are "wormholes" or invisible information tunnels between the sections of space-time. The wormholes transmit information instantaneously throughout the cosmos. The circulation of information is not regulated by the light-speed constant, as relativity theory insists, because such an alleged "barrier" to immediate translocation is solely a space-time effect. The universe may be an incredibly vast integrated circuit of concomitant information; or it may be an infinitely complex brain or nervous system in which information bundles are broadcast in rhythmic and self-organizing fashion throughout its intricate anatomy.

Such pulses are not necessarily "signals" in the conventional, cybernetic sense. Many physicists, however, have resisted the proposition that information can be propagated without some identifiable "carrier"; and they have fallen back on the surmise that information hitches onto a superluminal form of transport called *tachhyons* (from the Greek word for "speed"), which dart between space-time singularities, just as photons are exchanged between

[5] John Wheeler, "From Relativity to Mutability," in Jagdish Mehra (ed.), *The Physicist's Conception of Nature* (Dordrecht: D. Reidel, 1973), p. 238.

electrons in a magnetic field. The only difficulty with the tachyon thesis is that it seeks inadvertently to crowd the open-field paradigm of the new quantum theory into the cattle pen of corpuscular physics, which began its dissolution with quantum mechanics. The hypothesis also remains a sort of fossil causalism: it presumes there must be some tertiary agent that interposes between disparate events. Even Wheeler's suggestion of "wormholes" may hinge on the same sort of causalistic predilection. They may be like the concept of the "ether" in the nineteenth century, which was predicated on the not unreasonable inference that if light were indeed a wave form, it had to have a medium in which to travel.

Some historians have shown how many major hypotheses that seemed cogent at the time, but turned out subsequently to be chimeras, sprung from the persistence in the scientific community of metaphysical thought reflexes that belied the phenomenon under scrutiny. Thus the tendency of physicists to cling to the notion of the ether a hundred years ago may be explained by their long-standing inclination to ape Aristotle's *Posterior Analytics* in deeming that all change must have an underlying "substance." Likewise, the current fascination with the possibility of wormholes and tachyons may be little more than the aftershock of a way of thinking centering on bodies and causal relations between them.

A second prototype which eliminates many of the dead-ends and muddles of the wormhole construct has been drafted by Bohm. For Bohn, the problem of superluminal information transfer, as entiled in Bell's theorem and the concept of quantum inseparability, does not demand that one posit any kind of "information nexus" binding all events in other than a metaphorical sense. In Bohm's model information is not "translated" from one point to another in universal space, but is "stored" completely in each quantum of action. Or, to put the matter another way, every bit of information about the universe is "enfolded" into each particle or wave pattern as part of the implicate order. The implicate order is the plenum of all potentialities; it is the pattern of all possible patterns of action and change. Science, or human consciousness itself, can never descry the implicate order in its entirety. It can only exercise a piecemeal attention and actualize portions of the implicate reservoir from instant to instant. This process of selection and division owing to the inherent limits of human awareness is Bohm's explicate order— what each generation, civilization, or company of savants, including scientists, consture as reality.

Bohm's cosmology tallies in many respects with the metaphysics of Aristotle, for whom every "movement" (*kinesis*) is actualization of an indwelling "potential" (*dynamis*) and this formative process, or morphosis, is what makes a "thing." In addition, Aristotelian "causes" (*aitiai*) are not the goads of linear motion, as they are regarded in the push-pull prototype of Newtonian physics, but the "explicate" factors whereby what exists *in potentia* comes to be realized in the grand teleology of things.

Bohm cites his debt to Aristotle, in whose thought he contends "the order of movement as determined by the order of causes, which in turn depended on the place and function of each part in the whole."[6] Such a perspective, which Bohm dubs "holonomic," has a greater resemblance to the philosphy of Leibnitz whose cosmology quantum physics has rehabilitated and which Bohm lauds on several occasions. Leibniz' doctrine of "monads" draws within its ken the standpoint that (1) every part in some degree "mirrors" the whole (2) all action is the outworking of the inner drive of the monadic holon (3) the unique destiny of each singular intity participates in the intelligence and attuned to a "pre-established harmony." Leibniz himself asserted that

". . . the nature of the monad is representative, and consequently nothing can limit it to representing a part of things only, although it is true that its representation is confused as regards the detail of the whole universe and can only be distinct as regards a small part of things. . . ."[7]

Everything in itself reflects the macrocosm, although man's deficiency or "confusion" in his soul bars him from this splendid purview. Bohm's explication of a similar vision, however, draws less on Leibniz than on the physics of the hologram, a three-dimensional photography. Both Bohm and Wheeler have charted a cosmological perspective which *tout d'un coup* overhauls the syntax of normative philosophical discouse.

The breakthroughs of quantum physics, therefore, throws into a quite different light some abiding philosphical preconceptions concerning the road to scientific knowledge. The holonomic picture of reality, forged from the rule of quantum inscparability, calls into court many of the epistemological truisms that have steered modern reasoning and inquiry. Quantum inseparability is, on the main, a mathematical refinement of an older insight into the physics of field properties. It was foreshadowed, for example, in Mach's law which asserted that the mass of any particle is at some magnitude affected by the mass of all other particles in the universe. Later the theory of wave diffusion, coupled with a deepened understanding of the equivalence of mass and energy, gave rise to the conjecture that every "action" somehow becomes implicated with every other action in even the most faraway galaxies. But the quantum inseparability principle can also be considered an enlargement upon one of the rudimentary, yet telling discoveries of quantum mechanics. The reference is to Heisenberg's thesis that no experimenter can distinguish the observation from the observer, nor disentangle the measurement from the instrument. Heisenberg made his point with the case of electrons, although the disciples of Bell have subsequently generalized the same argument to instances of particle spin. Heisenberg noted that "elec-

[6]Bohm, p. 112.
[7]G. W. Leibniz, *Philosophical Writings*, trans. Mary Morris (New York: Dutton, 1968), p. 13.

trons", which from the beginning have remained experiential constructs, can never be seen as they are in themselves. Even if an intensely powerful microsope could be contrived to bring the electron into view, the energy from the light source would alter the path of the particle. The same restriction applies, albeit in a less overt manner, to all scientific observation and even everyday perceptions. Knower and known mutually condition each other. Therefore, Heisenberg concluded, we cannot really talk about the bald "object" to be observed, but only about the event of observation itself—Wheeler's moment of "observership."

On a larger scale it may be deduced that there can be no such thing as a self-existent universe whose "laws" progressively give way to intellectual probing. For the external and internal poles of consciousness cannot be segregated from each another. It makes no sense to speak of the "thing" apart from its manifestion within the orbit of universal intelligence.

At the same time, such an outlook does not, in contrast, justify subjective idealism. For the "subject" is as much a moment in the act of consciousness as the putative "object." Neither has epistemic priority. In this sense Bishop Berkeley was correct: "to be" is "to be perceived,." Yet "being perceived" does not amount to "I perceive." The "I" is as much an "illusion" in the mirror play of consciousness as the "other." The plumbline for gauging what is "real" can be neither the objective nor the subjective arc of vision. Both are complementary aspects, or distortions, of a more basic movement, as are Bohm's implicate and explicate orders. The new physics identifies this totality as *consciousness* pure and simple. But it is a consciousness that cannot be reduced to an attribute or affect of an individual subject. Thus it would be improper to draw theistic inferences, as some are wont to do, where this universal consciousness is interpreted as "the mind of God." Analogically speaking, perhaps we are all passing "thoughts" of the Creator. But that does not mean we are the "objective" content of his thought. For even under the aspect of eternity there can be no subject-object split. Religious considerations aside, the upshot of the new physics may be that the cosmos in both its inner and outer, or enfolded and unfolded, dimensions is in the strictest sense an infinite intelligence endeavoring to become "conscious of itself." The implication is strikingly Hegelian, and lights the way for theological thinking in its most profound aspects. As Wolf muses: "We have posed an answer to how it is that the fundamental act of life, the act of consciousness, by becoming aware of itself, in separation of I and not-I, changes itself. With each fundamental act, with myriads of twinkling star-like acts of awareness, the whole pattern forms and infinite lattice of connections between I and not-I twinkles. Laws of order and motions then appear as the least action strands in the cosmic spider web."[8]

The cosmic "spider web" of consciousness embraces within itself a

---

[8] Fred Wolf, "The Question of Parascience: A Physicist's View," in Bob Toben, *Space-Time and Beyond* (New York: Dutton, 1975), p. 158.

shoreless sea of open-ended relationships between what in one transitory glance may be viewed as "subjects" and with another blink as "objects." Insofar as all relations recoil upon each other, the universe may be called omnijective—woven with all trajectories of events. The transformations that take place within the omnijective universe, which at bottom is unbounded consciousness unfurling, become not the subject matter, but the very "soul" of science. The truth standards, as well as the particular themes, of science in a given era, are submerged within the universal process of self-explication. Scientific procedures can never "verify" hypotheses in a categorical sense, because verification is forever contingent on a finite project of thinking and investigation. Hegel anticipated quantum physics when, in the preface to his *Phenomenology of Spirit*, he wrote that "truth is the whole" and only the movement of infinite Spirit becoming cognizant of itself may count as "science."

Finally, even our much touted "empiricism" founders on these shoals, since sensation and observation are not necessarily more reliable than imagination or more encompassing "speculation." Quantum physics has come to appreciate with renewed acumen the ancient Hellenic subordination of *aisthesis* (sensation) to *noesis* (intellection). The modern exaltation of sense data at the expense of what the Greeks called "forms" or "ideas" has led to the improvement of science in both its utility and theory. Yet it has also robbed science of its transcendental sweep and contributed to the fallacy of what Bernard d'Espagant terms "multitudinism", the pretense that real things are most intelligible when they are differentiated and compartmentalized, rather when they are studied in their unitary dimension. As Plato recognized, sense experience is intrisically fragmentary, even if the method of inductive validation is retailed as descriptive metaphysics, as we find in the empiricist tradition from Locke to Russell. Empiricism, as we have claimed, is the colossal "superstition" of our time in the sense of the Latin *superstitio*, which means "that which binds or narrows one's attention." The empiricist superstition has promoted the reification of what are merely sensory, or more precisely *con-sensual*, representations, of what neurophysiologists term "afferent inputs". Our "hard data" may be little more than lazy abstractions. In a word, quantum physics leads us away from a constricting, contentious, and reifying science toward a window on the omnijective universe. But the wholeless of a quantum interconnected omniject can become a pernicious abstraction, or a mystical shibboleth, if we are not careful. What is required is an epistemology which will yield, as it did for Kant, a "transcendental" philosophy or a critical metaphysics. Theological thinking may appropriate the world vision of quantum theory in the measure that it seeks to unchain itself from the modern superstition of the given. But it must beware of reifying the new perspective, lest it become the font for a new obscurantism that loses the sense of the distinction between what is simply unfathomable and what glitters like a golden calf in the intellectual imagination.

CHAPTER 7

EVOLUTION AND THE ESCHATON: THEOLOGICAL USES AND ABUSES OF THE NEW SCIENCE

"Humanity has in the course of time had to endure from the hands of science two great outrages upon its naive self-love. The first was when it realized that our earth was not the center of the universe, but only a tiny speck in a world-system of a magnitude hardly conceivable; this is associated in our minds with the name of Copernicus . . . The second was when biological research robbed man of his peculiar privilege of having been specially created, and relegated him to a descent from the animal world, implying an ineradicable animal nature in him: this transvaluation has been accomplisted in our own time upon the instigation of Charles Darwin . . . But man's craving for grandiosity is now suffering the third and most bitter blow from present-day psychological research which is endeavoring to prove in his own house . . . We psycho-analysts were neither the first nor the only ones to propose to mankind that they should look inward. . ."

—SIGMUND FREUD

The foregoing quote from Freud, who may be considered the last great "critical" philosopher in the post-Enlightenment disassembly of doctrinal faith, contains implications which regular exegesis is likely to miss. The present day assimilation of theology to psychology leaves us in a quandry. Victorian science succeeded in toppling Scriptural authority and enthroning the notion of our "ineradicable animal nature". Humanity's feral genesis, as documented by Darwin, found its logical end point in the postulate of the species' profound beastly constitution, according to Freud's topological model of the unconscious. The quasi-mythic ape-man envisioned by nineteenth century paleontology became enshrined in the psychoanalytic discourse elaborated from the Freudian constructs of "libido" and "id."

Darwin's own "biohermeneutic" at the conclusion of *The Origin of Species*, according to which "genealogies" rather than taxonomies would "be called the plan of creation",[1] prefigured Freud's own fatalism. It is humanity's "memories of the helplessness of his own childhood and the childhood of the

---

[1] See Charles Darwin, *The Origin of Species* (New York: Penguin Books, 1976), p. 456.

human race", Freud argued, that gave birth to the "store of [religious] ideas."[2] Our modernist obsession with deposing and "deconstituting" our own traditions has left us heedless toward our ideological motives. But we must also acknowledge that the nineteenth century critique of ideology, which emerged with Marx and Nietzsche, was actually a kind of pious pilgrimage back to beginnings, a quest for the holy grail of "consciousness." "Truthfulness", as Nietzsche put it, was prior both conceptually and temporally to the religious "lie." And truthfulness could only be sought in what we might call humanity's palingenesis, erasing Western theology's prepossession with God as "wholly other", which Nietzsche blamed on the "Jewish" character of Christianity as a religion, if not Jesus personally.

The palingenesis would be accomplished not by science in the abstract, but by what turned out to be a curious, modern pseudo-Hermetic *scientia* in which all knowledge of ultimate things would have to take an "inward turn." The theory of evolution was not so much a scientific doctrine as it was a heuristics for piecing together a new metaphysics of humanity. Darwin's finches were merely the proof positive for speculations already erected by Kant and Herder, and a montage of now mostly forgotten flag bearers of the Romantic movement. The long-standing dogma of creation was now recast by the self-same Romantics as the mystique of unfolding sentience, what Hegel at the conclusion of his *Phenomenology* dubbed "the revelation of the depth of Spirit."[3] Hegel's "revelation" was, in fact, not an eschatology but a novel, philosophical recapitulation of Genesis in which the great arc of time was now completed.

Evolutionism, like the kindred doctrine of historicism, arose in the nineteenth century as a "post-Christian" means of sanctifying time without resorting to teleology. In one respect evolutionism may be construed as a desperate kind of solution to an inherent contradiction in the post-Newtonian physical sciences. Classical physics, as one writer observes, singled out "the special status of inertia as an essential property of material substance."[4] Motion was merely the result of a body's displacement by an applied force. Dynamic changes—which in all metaphysics prior to Descartes had been regulated by Aristotelian entelechies—were now conceived as the effect of linear reactions. The Great Chain of Being had become the vast panorama of process.

But evolutionism in the long haul did breed its own wry kind of teleology. And that teleology was a turning upside down of the Christian notion

[2] Sigmund Freud, *The Future of an Illusion*, trans. W. D. Robson-Scott (Garden City, NY: Doubleday, 1964), p. 25.
[3] G. W. F. Hegel, *Phenomenology of Spirit*, trans. A. V. Miller (New York: Oxford University Press, 1977), p. 492.
[4] P. M. Harman, *Metaphysics and Natural Philosophy* (Sussex, NJ: The Harvester Press, 1982), p. 13.

of providence. Its elaboration coincided—but not "coincidentally"—with
Nietzsche's annunciation of Europe's "nihilism." Proclaimed Nietzsche: "Without the Christian faith," Pascal thought, "you, no less than nature
and history, will become for yourselves *un monstre et un chaos.*" This
prophecy we have fulfilled, after the feeble-optimistic eighteenth century
had prettified and rationalized man.[5] The *monstre et un chaos* reared up in
classical physics' own closet with the development of the theory of entropy.
Formulated by Ludwig Boltzmann, the postulate of entropy referred to the
tendency of closed, thermodynamic systems to become disorganized. The
tendency toward disorganization, as it happened, had little to do with the
classical emphasis on motion. It threw in relief for the first time since the
eclipse of Scholasticism the factor of what we know term "information". And
the late nineteenth century renaissance of information theory may be seen as
a recoil against Newton's censoring of teleology, especially since the empirical demands on evolutionary naturalism could not be met without such a
rectification. Evolutionism and classical thermodynamics share a similar
metaphysical pedigree. They cannot be segregated any more than special
relativity and four dimensional geometry, even though the latter, for instance, were advanced by Einstein and Minkowski with different motines in
mind.

These excurses in the history of science are intended mainly to highlight
a new and comparable type of interrelationship between biology, physics,
and religious psychology, which is gaining ground today and makes Freud's
case as best as can be conceived. The reference here is to the scientific field
known as "non-equilibrium thermodynamics" or, philosophically speaking,
as "systems theory". The most prominent advances in the field have come
through the Noble Prize-winning research of Ilya Prigogine, and they have
been interpreted philosophically in the work of Erich Jantsch. The theories
of Prigogine, unfortunately, are often quite formidable for the non-specialist,
especially in the humanities, because he usually chooses to couch them in a
high-level mathematical formalism. Prigogine's theories center on the notion
of "dissipative structures." Dissipative structures are best understood in the
context of cybernetics or "systems dynamics." They are the outcome of an
equilibration of influx and efflux ("input" and "output" in the language of
information theory), resulting in a discrete kind of patterning or "form." The
"self-organization" of energy into *Gestalten* under certain conditions runs
counter to the second law of thermodynamics and accounts for local
negentropic moments in time's current which we perceive as "life."

There is, however, nothing mysterious or "vitalistic" about living organisms, according to Prigogine. Their morphic properties are the simple consequence of what in systems theory is termed "steady state" or, as the

---

[5] Friedrich Nietzsche, *The Will to Power*, trans. Walter Kaufmann (New York: Random House, 1967), pp. 51–52.

German equivalent *Fliessgleichgewicht* connotes, "balance of flow." Self-patterning flux vectors are defined by the values of negentropy, because they occur in open systems, whereas thermodynamic finality is an outgrowth of processes in closed systems.

Prigogine's "new" biochemistry, therefore, represents for the most part a transposition of the assumptions of the older mechanico-materialism from an atomistic to a holistic reference frame. As Prigogine himself states: "our basic postulate is that all vital phenomena can be studied with reference to both the laws of physics appropriate to the specific nonlinear interactions we have to consider and to the far-from-equilibrium conditions."[6] The phrasing "far from equilibrium" is the cue. Unlike the older thermodynamics, Prigogine's work demonstrates that order and maximum probability—the parameters of what is mathematically known as "entropy"—are not necessarily synonymous. Maximum probablity of possible states occurs when there is minimal energy exchange between the components of a system. But, according to Prigogine, it is only when a system is in a high flux and thereby "unstable" can the negentropic characteristics of organic entities emerge. Comments Prigogine: "One of our conclusions is that there exist systems showing two types of behavior, namely, a tendency to a disordered state under certain conditions and a coherent behavior under others. The destruction of order prevails in the neighborhood of thermodynamic equilibrium. Creation of order may occur far from equilibrium provided the system obeys to nonlinear laws of a certain type."[7] Hence, the explanation for biogenesis cannot be couched in terms of linear and real-time mutations, but only with regard to orthogonal or multi-variable processes that seem strangely "intelligent."

These processes, however, are indwelling in nature. According to Jeremy Campbell, "[Prigogine] believes that organized systems arise naturally out of unorganized matter rather than being extraordinary flukes or arriving on the earth from elsewhere in the universe. He proposes the existence of a hitherton unrecognized principle which pushes living organisms, even human beings themselves, to states of greater and greater complexity, whether or not that is the direction in which they want to go."[8]

Prigogine, therefore, has given us what amounts to a non-religious cosmogony in which creativity transpires in the midst of chaos. Even the accumulation of entropy is necessary, for Prigogine, in order to spur dynamic change. To put the matter in a more familiar mythopoetic diction: the threat

[6] G. Nicolis and I. Prigogine, *Self-Organization in Nonequilibrium Systems: From Dissipative Structures to Order Through Fluctuations* (New York: John Wiley Sons, 1977), p. 21.

[7] Nicolis and Priogine, p. 25.

[8] Jeremy Campbell, *Grammatical Man: Information, Entropy, Language, and Life* (New York: Simon & Schuster, 1982), pp. 100–1.

of death invariably enhances life. Or, as Prigogine enunciates the same idea
in a technical fashion, "a complete change in perspective has arisen, and we
begin to understand the constructive role play be irreversible processes in
the physical world."[9] Vitalism, or even more orthodox instances of "crea-
tionism", become superfluous by this reckoning. "Life," asserts Prigogine,
"no longer appears as an island of resistance against the second law of
thermodynamics . . . It would appear now as a consequence of the general
laws of physics, appropriate to specific chemical kinetics . . . which permit
the flow of energy and matter to build and maintain functional and structural
order in open systems."[10] Both the upshot and general application of Prigogine's observations hinge upon the inference that the biostratum as a
whole is "divine" (i.e., endued with some noetic capacity). We are reminded, of course, of the ancient Stoic opinion concerning an ingrained
logos spermatikos throughout the universe.

Yet the entailment may be even stronger. In Prigogine we are possibly
closer to the hieratic imagery of "the twilight of the gods." The invocation is
to Nietzsche's Zarathustra: "I show you a death that consummates."[11] Or do
we discern here a physicalist foundation for a "Dionysian" metaphysics of
decadence. On that score we must quote James Ogilvy from his *Many
Dimensional Man:* "the life that is sacred is the life lived in the presence of
death and rebirth . . ."[2] Systems biophysics yields the (ostensibly) morally
inconsequential position that, in the words of Jantsch, "an open system far
from equilibrium . . . is driven by fluctuations across one or more instability
thresholds and enters a new co-ordinated phase of its evolution."[13] However,
the metaphysical innuendoes are striking. Creation is assimilated not to the
holy word of Hebrew tradition, but to the Indo-Aryan primal sacrifice
outlined in the *Rig Veda.* It is violence— especially a violence against what
can be contextually identified as "moral" order—that lies at the core of
cosmic novelty. Thus we are thrown back in assent to one of Nietzsche's more
bluff, hyperbolic, and uncharacteristically candid passages: We sail right over
morality, we crush, we destroy perhaps the remains of our own morality by
daring to make the voyage there . . . Never yet did a profounder world of
insight reveal itself to daring travelers and adventurers, and the psychologist

[9] Ilya Prigogine, *From Being to Becoming: Time and Complexity in the Physical Sciences* (San Francisco, CA: W. H. Freeman, 1980), p. 78.

[10] P. Glansdorff and I. Prigogine, *Thermodynamic Theory of Structure, Stability and Fluctuations* (London: Wiley-Interscience, 1971), p. 289.

[11] Friedrich Nietzsche, ,"Thus Spoke Zarathustra," in Walter Kaufmann (ed.), *The Portable Nietzsche* (New York: Random House, 1967), p. 182.

[12] James Ogilvy, *Many Dimensional Man: Decentralizing Self, Society, and the Sacred* (New York: Harper & Row, 1979), p. 171.

[13] Erich Jantsch, *The Self-Organizing Universe: Scientific and Human Implications of the Emerging Paradigm of Evolution* (New York: Pergamon Press, 1980), p. 73.

who thus "makes a sacrifice . . . will at least be entitled to demand in return
that psychology shall be recognized again as the queen of the sciences . . .
For psychology is now again the path to the fundamental problems."[14]

Theology, which Nietzsche always took as a camouflage for "morality",
by this reckoning must collapse into psychology. For it is the psyche—as it
was for ancient paganism—that is embedded as the vivifying power of
nature. The psyche is replenished through the agonism of sacrifice and
mutilation. Such is the inherent rationale for all magic. In the sacral imma-
nentism of the new systems science we have, curiously, the formality of an
archaic and pre-Christian mythos. Can its ethos remain disguised for very
long?

The overshadowing of present day natural science by particle physics
and quantum theory has brought us to a curious ideological pass. No scientific world view can crystallize in any era without generating encompassing
mind sets at both the subliminal and "common sense" level that mimic it in
some way. The two tend to arise in tandem with each other, as Michel
Foucault has recognized in his analysis of the historical *episteme*. The more
abstruse conceptual architecture of, say, a Prigogine or Ludwig Bertallanfy—
the patriarch of systems thinking—acquired its popular semiology with the
advent over a decade earlier of Capra's "new physics," which superimposed
on the model now known as "chaos dynamics" the philosophical lexicon of
quantum mechanics. Capra noted: "The exploration of the subatomic world
in the twentieth century has revealed the intrinsically dynamic of matter
nature of matter. It has shown that the constituents of atoms, the subatomic
particles, are dynamic patterns which do not exist as isolated entities, but as
integral parts of an inseparable network of interactions. These interactions
involve a ceaseless flow of energy manifesting itself as the exchange of
particles . . ."[15]

Capra's volume, which set forth in the popular context more than any
other trade book the master analogues and essential images behind the new
physics, was in hindsight more tendentious than it appeared at the time. For
quantum theory and submolecular research has always remained metaphysically ambiguous. Karl Popper, the last great positivist, warned only
recently that "today, physics is in a crisis" on account of "the intrusion of
subjectivism into [the discipline]."[16] The red flag of "subjectivism," of course
may be casually tossed out to denigrate all non-empirical statements. But
Popper has a point in admonishing against the sort of psychospiritual reductionism that has dominated commercial presentations of physics after Ein-

[14] Friedrich Nietzsche, *Beyond Good and Evil*, trans. Walter Kaufmann (New York: Random
House, 1966), pp. 31–2.
[15] See Fritjof Capra, above.
[16] Karl Popper, *Quantum Theory and the Schism in Physics* (Totowa, NJ: Rowman and
Littlefield, 1982), p. 1.

stein. It was, after all, Eugene Wigner who first resolved the dilemma of observer-dependence in the realization of experimental eigenstates by positing an alchemy of "consciousness." But Wigner did not mean—as many of his "New Age" interpreters have been wont to presume as well as trumpet—that individual, subjective intention (after the fashion of the sorcerer's concentration of willpower) is responsible for what in technical jargon is termed the "collapse of the state vector."

The persistent association of scientific inquiry with occultism has been subtle, yet pervasive. The major premise of occultism or Gnostic esotericism has been that intelligibility derives from immanent or sublunary forms and processes. Henceforth, there is a distinct, anti-Hebraic agenda in the popularization of quantum mechanics. There is also a quiet and implicit anarcho-mysticism. I quote Capra: "[particle physics] not only denies the existence of fundamental constituents of matter, but accepts no fundamental entities whatsoever—no fundamental laws, equations or principles—and thus abandons another idea which has been an essential part of natural science for hundreds of years. The notion of fundamental laws of nature was derived from the belief in a divine Lawgiver which was deeply rooted in the Judaeo-Christian tradition."[17] Capra's "Buddhist" version of the bootstrap theory in particle physics is cognate on many levels with non-equilibrium thermodynamics, inasmuch as it maintains that order and creativity are "spontaneous" products of random flux through which ephemeral particle assemblies cohere and dissolve as in the Mahayana concept of "dependent co-origination." But we must ask ourselves in all candor: what is the significant philosophical and theological outcome of our current fascination with the new sciences, particularly the peculiar school of systems biophysics that has had a great impact on liberal religious thought? The same liberal outlook has been seeking all along to divest itself of all attachment to Christian monotheism and affirm some blurred pluralistic ontology which is, strangely, a species of "spiritual materialism"—a philosophical overview, as physicist David Bohm expresses it, of "matter in which life and intelligence are immanent and implicit."[18] We should twist the question around somewhat differently and ask: what is the endpoint of the "way of immanence" that begins not in Benares but at Gologotha? What is the present trajectory of an Occidental "evolutionism" which has attempted to blot out the glintings of a transcendent Lord of history while dangling the lure of science qua spirit? In answer we must look more carefully at the writings of Thomas J. J. Altizer.

Altizer, who is generally considered the progenitor of the "death of God" movement nearly two decades ago, disclosed the incipient meaning of that

[17] Capra, p. 286.
[18] David Bohm, "The Physicist and the Mystic—Is a Dialogue Between Them Possible?", in Ken Wilber (ed.), *The Holographic Paradigm and Other Paradoxes: Exploring the Leading Edge of Science* (Boulder, CO: Shambhala, 1982), p. 193.

strident historical parenthesis as follows: "the death of God in Christ is an inevitable consequence of the movement of God into the world, of Spirit into flesh . . . a self-negating and kenotic movement, as both embodied and symbolically enacted in the passion of Christ . . . manifest in the suffering and darkness of a naked human experience, an experience banished from the garden of innocence, and emptied of the sustaining power of a transcendent ground or source."[19]

Here we have the conclusion of Hegel's *Phenomenology* where "apocalypse" becomes endless history, "Spirit emptied out into time." And the assimilation of eternity to the temporal, of infinity to the finite, of supersenible Deity to a spectrum of utter "worldliness", of religion to "science", of wholly otherness to "total presence," generates a pure identity—Nicholas of Cusa's *coincidentia oppositorum*—in which eschatology truly becomes Nietzsche's Dionysian deluge of immanence. In Altizer's vision there can be no separation between Good Friday and Easter, between the Cross and salvation. For passion and triumph become unitary. The Johannine declaration "I am the resurrection and the life" makes sense, proclaims Altizer, "only when life and death are one."[20] The overtones, of course, are unmistakably Cybelean. Religion is transfigured from worship into theater—Artaud's "theater of cruelty". The "Christian" experience, riveted on what is interminably cruciform, now is bared as a self-conscious and global anti-Christianity. The language is Altizer's own: "therefore the Christian is finally called to accept the Antichrist, or the totality of the dead body of God, as a final kenotic manifestation of Christ . . . we must nevertheless be prepared to open ourselves to the anguish and terror of experience as an expression of the atoning process of redemption, a process that even now is unveiling a yet fuller form of horror by dissolving the sacred and transcendent masks of experience, and actualizing experience in a totally immanent form."[21] And perhaps does not this "horror" of immanence, celebrated by Altizer in his sepulchral rhapsodies, betoken some sort of unprecedented fusion of hermeneutical horizons—in this instance, the technological and the sacerdotal. The cybernetic mimesis of Prigogine's dissipative formations, the codification of the Dionysian dithyramb as "science," would bring about Altizer's eschatology of "our own interior and individual dissolution as the way to the realization of our own full and universal humanity."[22]

Altizer's expectation of our "own interior and individual dissolution", therefore, projects one phase further the evolutionistic thrust encapsulated by Freud at the outset of our discussion. The "inward turn" of science, and

[19]Thomas J. J. Altizer, *The Gospel of Christian Atheism* (Philadelphia: The Westminster Press, 1966), p. 122.

[20]Thomas J. J. Altizer, *The Self-Embodiment of God* (New York: Harper & Row, 1977), p. 91.

[21]*Gospel of Christian Atheism*, p. 122.

[22]Thomas J. J. Altizer, *Total Presence: The Language of Jesus and the Language of Today* (New York: Seabury, 1980), p. 88.

even axiology, that became quite evident with psychoanalysis has perhaps reached its climax in our current *denouement* of nihilism, what Altizer himself dubs the "solitude of the end." Mentalism and mechanism are disclosed as having a common center of gravity—the same "Tao" as it were— rather than their former semblance of a polarity. The machine in a godless world without a skylight to heaven becomes a simulacrum for creativity. The Golem is nought but the parabolic equivalent of our preoccupation with bioengineering arrayed around the technics of dissipative structures.

In the words of Norbert Wiener, forbear of the computer revolution, "the machine, like the living organism, is . . . a device which locally and temporarily seems to resist the general tendency for the increase of entropy. By its ability to make decisions it can produce around it a local zone of organization in a world whose general tendency is to run down."[23] If humanity is the last recourse against entropy in a universe that has a temporal momentum, but not a providential direction, what is the ethical legacy that we may foresee? According to Steven M. Stanley, who offers his own "punctuationalist" account of evolution adduced from Prigogine's physical chemistry in contest with both Christian orthodoxy and natural selection, the answer is "cultural governance of our biological evolution" that is "closely similar . . . to our genetic engineering of other species."[24] A cosmically framed Promethean defiance is conspicuous in such a sensibility.

The new science has the potential to be a ladder to heaven, or a latter day Tower of Babel. We can only avoid its becoming a Tower of Babel if we scrupulously eschew the urge toward reification. We must renounce the liberal penchant for making the critical tendencies of the new science the basis of a new metaphysics. The metaphysical drive that inheres in all forms of theological thinking, and is most pronounced when it leans toward the scientific side, can only be compensated in the final analysis by a cultivated hermeneutical consciousness.

[23] Norbert Wiener, *The Human Use of Human Beings* (New York: Avon Books, 1967), p. 49.
[24] Steven M. Stanley, *The New Evolutionary Timetable* (New York: Basic Books, 1981), p. 206.

SECTION III

HERMENEUTICS

CHAPTER 8

HERMENEUTICAL THINKING

"Thought is the proper use of reason moving from those things
which are certain to those things which are uncertain."
—SAINT AUGUSTINE

The tendency of scientific thinking to reify its mythic vistas and to generate a metaphysics with its own seductive formalities runs counter, however, to the theological spirit of innovation. The quest for innovation in theological thinking, as we shall see, is born of the penetrating force behind the questions and conjectures of those who would be, in the most ancient sense, "God-seekers." Since the emergence of liberal theology in the nineteenth century, the drive for innovation has generally been carried by the desire to accomodate the Christian "proclamation" to the often incompatible demands of what in effect has been a neo-pagan cultural milieu. Post-Newtonian science itself has been the crucible and forge for the development of this new milieu. Religious liberalism has tended to follow the changing of the milieu in the same way that women of the night in eras bygone used to pursue army bivouacs. The danger always lies, therefore, in a disposition of theological thinking to prostrate itself before the idols of the age.

Yet, at the same time, the spirit of innovation has been constantly whetted by the pressure for "revision" of our traditional theological understanding, even if the outcome is frequently a diminution of that very understanding. Innovation requires interpretation, and what we find in the liberal setting is a requirement of an ongoing interpretative stance that mediates between revelation and culture, or to use the classic locutions, between *logos* and *nomos*. A "theo-logy" that refuses to enter into conversation with cultural and historical presumptions is empty, just as any theological endeavor which simply relies on the alterity of certain cultural and intellectual preoccupations for its own self-critique is blind and feckless. Interpretation is not merely the systematic mediation between amalgams of signs, as the post-structuralist fashion in contemporary semiotic theory encourages us to believe. Nor is it only a synthesis of outlooks, the so-called "fusion of horizons" declared by Gadamer. Interpretation is fundamentally a moment of disclosure, not to mention a recovery. Invariably it has an archaeological dimension. That is why Freud, who truly blazed the way for present day "hermeneutical" theory, as opposed to historicist, linguistic, or sociologistic reductions of textual materials, could say categorically: "interpreting means finding a hidden sense in something."[1] But when we speak of the "hidden sense" of the hermeneutical situation, are we referring merely to a buried signification that somehow already exists within the normative grammar of the text under consideration, or are pointing up a genuinely unthought, or "unsaid," reservoir of meaning. Freud definitely thought the latter, spurring him to postulate the notion of an "unconscious" mind, which could only be made intelligible through the most strange kind of metalogical explication using such ambiguous hermeneutical constructs as "transference," "displacement," and "condensation."

The object lesson of Freud's larger "metapsychological" effort, which increasingly has come to be ridiculed for its lack of empirical foundations, is that interpretation itself demands that we move concertedly from our given, self-certifying historical epistemology to one which cannot be so easily enunciated. This shadow epistemology, which compels the hermeneutical task by the very fact that it is not ready to grasp and self-certifying, makes interpretation possible in the first place. The opaque sense of the text, of the dream, or of any psychic or cultural artifact for that matter, belongs to the shadow epistemology. But the actual interpretation, like the epistemology itself, must arise from the passage of thought beyond its own boundaries into terrain of the unknown, or the unthought. In this regard the hermeneutical object is comparable to a virtual particle in high energy physics. Its virtuality is confirmed by what is seen or observed, but its existence only makes sense in terms of what it is not. The virtual particle has a "hidden sense" in relation to what does not make sense from the standpoint of the regular observer. Similarly, in hermeneutics the shadow form of the object must be both derived and constituted in order to elucidate the dilemmas posed by the attempt to understand the object in itself.

So long as theological thinking is confined, as it has for the most part since the Middle Ages, to the "God object" circumscribed within canon, tradition, and selected gleanings from Scripture (i.e. Aquinas' *doctrina sacra*), it has preserved its consistency at the expense of its depth, and hence of its significance. A theology aimed at the "depths" of both language and the world—what we have heretofore dubbed "batho-theology"—is not a cultural theology with all the implications that term carries, but a form of theological thinking that glorifies what the Israelites knew as the Lord Almighty in all his wisdom. Such a version of theological thinking can best be described as "hermeneutical", although as we have already stressed, it goes far beyond the renderings of specific texts. Hermeneutical theology, or more appropriately a theological thinking that is hermeneutically grounded, strives irre-

---

[1] Sigmund Freud, *Introductory Lectures on Psychoanalysis*, trans. James Strachey (New York: W. W. Norton, 1966), p. 87.

pressibly for the recovery of what is unthought. Its concern is not merely the hidden sense of the *verba divina* that appear in the guise of antique documents, but the creative "word" that manifests itself through the archives, leavings, and sundry objectivities of history and culture.

The vigor of early modern theology and science together was drawn from a belief, blazoned during the Renaissance and late appropriated by Calvinist intellectuals, especially in England, that the natural world is eminently the sphere of God's self-disclosure, that the "book of nature" should be read almost as avidly as the Holy Book itself.[2] What the early moderns termed "natural philosophy," therefore, was originally shaped by an abiding hermeneutical interest—a quest for the meaning of what was concealed everywhere in God's creation. But the scientific aim can only be regarded as hermeneutical in a limited sense, for it asks that the seeker, or observer, set about his work with a well-honed purpose in mind. In the seventeenth century the concrete outcome of this hermeneutics of nature, even as Bacon with his quasi-occultist leanings had defined it, was "experiment".[3] Experimental science in this period, henceforth, can construed as the practical hermeneutics of an ever influential natural theology. It was the *applicatio*, if we may refer back to Medieval models of interpretation, of the received sense of the "text" itself.

If the seventeenth century had looked upon nature as the essential compendium of divine enigmas, by the late 1700s and early nineteenth century the focus has shifted to human civilization and historical life. The proliferation of the so-called "human sciences" during this era can be explained by a miscellany of factors, including the burgeoning of democratic sentiments and the opening of Europe through trade and colonialism to a spectrum of alien cultures. German Romanticism with its grand notion of history as the theater of mysterious spiritual energies and forces became the ideological seedbed for this new interest. Philosophical "hermeneutics", which under the influence of Wilhelm Dilthey sought to probe into the entire "life" enveloping authors and books, came to perform a crucial function in the transition from what was fundamentally a theology of glory to a new, immanentist, and world historical version of Luther's *theologia crucis*. We find the philosophical underpinnings for such a changeover in the thought of J. G. Herder, who adapted Spinoza's classic pantheism to the Romantic vision itself. Just as Spinoza, by his turgid method of geometric demonstration, had shown that the traditional, philosophical concept of God

---

[2] For a detailed exposition of how this view could be found in the writings of such early pioneers in science as Boyle, Locke, and Glanville, see Richard S. Westfall, *Science and Religion in Seventeenth-Century England* (New Haven, CN: Yale University Press, 1958), p. 26ff.

[3] Although scholars are still divided on the issue, it appears that a good deal of Bacon's language of experimentalism is adapted from Renaissance hermeticism.

an *ens perfectissiumu,* or "most perfect being," must logically entail his co-extension with nature, Herder argued that "the highest Power can be nothing but the highest Wisdom and Goodness eternally-living, eternally-active," which includes his presence in the minute workings of history. For Herder, God is ". . . active in the smallest and in the largest, in every point of space and time, that is, in every living force of the universe . . . The whole world is an expression, an appearance of his eternally-living, eternally-active forces."[4] At the same time, Herder was no garden variety pantheist. The ganglion of divine energy and activity, according to Herder, is to be found in the historical momentum of the human species; and the focal point of God's never-ceasing creative efforts is the formation, or "education", of the race itself. Says Herder: "God made man a deity upon Earth; he implanted in him the principle of self-activity, and set this principle in motion from the beginning, by means of the internal and external wants of his nature."[5] History, therefore, is a gigantic wall of runes, a portal to incalculable mysteries decorated with the hieroglyphs of what Herder termed the "imagination." Speaking from the hermeneutical standpoint, we may say that historical consciousness, as well as historical *res gestae,* are the intricately and delicately limned annals of God in the fullness of his own experience and sensibility. The Hegelian concept of historical progress as the outworking of the Holy Spirit itself was extracted from this expansive historico-theism, which became the very foundation of faith for numerous generations of political theorists, anthropologists, philologist, and students of "world religions." The book of history as a whole, not simply the "sacred book" of the Israelites, was viewed as open to the art of interpretation. Hermeneutical science was transposed from a theological into a "humanistic" discipline. Yet the theological undertones of historical inquiry did not vanish. Theological thinking became a genuine bathotheology, insofar as it was now bidden to explore, sift, and appraise the vast-ranging depths of all life, past and present. The thoroughgoing rationality of the whole of historical existence, denied since antiquity, came to be asserted as the fundamental datum of the new cultural hermeneutics. Freud's later attempt to delve into the pathologies of ordinary personalities by concocting a "metapsychology", which presupposed a strangely coded unconscious heritage extending back to prehistory, was but a clinical refinement of the Romantic attitude. In fact, the hermeneutical preoccupation of so much twentieth century theology, commencing with Bultmann, may be viewed as the inevitable consequence of this shift, which took place almost a century earlier.

The point to be enforced here, of course, is that theological thinking in

[4]Johann Gottfried Herder, *God, Some Conversations,* trans. Frederick H. Budkhardt (Indianapolis: Bobbs-Merrill, 1940), p. 170.
[5]J. G. Herder, *Reflections on the Philosophy of the History of Mankind* (Chicago: University of Chicago Press, 1968), p. 84.

the late modern era rapidly came to be distinguished by its preoccupation with historical variation and change. The irony is that while the original motive of historicist reflection was a longing to behold the face of God amidst the contingencies of human culture and innovation, its eventual commitment was to reject the unity of the divine presence in deference to the lush relativity of religious forms and practices. What has recently devolved into a bland and sociologically tinted litter of empirical observations without a conceptual substratum was once a proud, theological position. The difficulty faced almost from the beginning by such a history-minded depth theology was a plausible format within which the seemingly inexhaustible surface features of the phenomenon in question might be separated from the fundamental structure of meaning. If every element of the historical process was benignly providential, in contrast to say the classic, Pauline and Augustinian perspectives from which the elect alone could be said to be directly accomplishing God's projects, then useful rules of discrimination were hard to come by. The hermeneutical search for God's signatures within history swiftly passed over into a promiscuous adoration of historical life itself. The so-called "secular" obsession of contemporary Protestantism can be perceived as the long-term outgrowth of these developments.

The leading difference between modern and classical hermeneutics is that while the latter struggled to identify the transcendent or supernal value of religious passages, the former has consistently endeavored to uncover its immanent, including its peripheral and strictly contextual, significations. Most of contemporary hermeneutics, therefore, could be assimilated to the Medieval concern with finding the "literal" sense of the text. Classical Christian hermeneutical theory was always an adjunct to theology, which in turn was ineradicably supernaturalistic in its leanings. The genuine, or spiritual, meaning of a piece of Scripture was derived not from history, but from doctrine—what might somewhat whimsically be termed, using our own mode of anology, the "book of teaching." In the Middle Ages itself the function of hermeneutics was linked immediately to monastic edification. It was part of what was known as the *lectio divina*, the discourse specifically on what is ultimate, otherworldly, and holy.[6]

Starting with the Romantic era, however, hermeneutics was disconnected from its theological roots and grafted on to the nascent, independent discipline of literary criticism. How this changeover actually resulted remains somewhat obscure, but suffice it to say that the Romantic metaphysics of the imagination, elaborated by such figures as Coleridge, Schelling, and

---

[6] For an account of the relationship between hermeneutics and doctrinal theology, see Heiko A. Oberman, *The Harvest of Medieval Theology* (Grand Rapids, MI: William B. Eerdmans, 1967). Oberman notes that in the Medieval setting "the structure of biblical theology is never higher than the single step from the particular passage to its doctrinal meaning." (pp. 74–5). Analysis of the *lectio divina* is found in Beryl Smalley, *The Study of the Bible in the Middle Ages* (Notre Dame: University of Notre Dame Press, 1964), p. 88f.

Novalis, was instrumental in altering the semantics of divine action in a decisive manner.[7] No longer was the "faith" given by the Holy Spirit, or what in Medieval circles had been known as *fides infusa*, an intelligible notion in the defense of the religious standpoint. It was the prime contribution of the Romantic thinkers to psychologize religion in a radical way, and the upshot was a transposing of the orthodox language of spiritual inspiration into the syntax of imaginative "genius." The saint was now the artist, the ascetic the Bohemian, the monk the essayist. By the Victorian period this belief had become domesticated as part of the piety of liberal Protestantism. To read the Bible was to read the immortal truths of great literature, as evinced in the sentiment of Matthew Arnold that Scriptural hermeneutics requires "culture, the acquainting ourselves with the best that has been known and said in the world, and thus with the history of the human spirit."[8] With the rise of experimental psychology the "problem" of interpretation became a broader issue within the very domain of epistemology; it became inextricably bound up with Kant's rudimentary question of how knowledge is possible in the first place.

The great "hermeneutical turn" in modern arts and letters may be regarded as an omnibus response to the unsolved dilemmas of Kant himself. The central Kantian category of the "thing in itself," which has continually vexed idealists and positivists alike, stakes out the boundary zone between pure epistemology and the precise science of interpretation. Since Kant at least, epistemological reflection has been caught up with the consideration of the constraints upon what we can both assert and understand. Kant himself designated the "thing in itself" as a "limiting concept," as a kind of phantom object which, when analyzed, vanishes into the essential realization it is the conditions of subject knowledge that shape our judgements. Hermeneutics, at the same time, looks to disclose the absent object, the *mysterium* lurking behind the iconic material that requires interpretation. Whereas epistemology remains discrete and backs off from engaging the alterity of what is stated, written, or depicted, hermeneutics intends to pierce the veil of secrecy. The virtue of epistemology is intellectual chastity. The force of the hermeneutical drive is toward a seduction of the unthought contents of the proposition, or linguistic situation. The so-called "critical philosphy" of Kant made overlarge the task of philosophical hermeneutics, because for the first time within the Western tradition, excluding perhaps the brief interlude of Medieval nominalism, it thoroughly befogged the rules of both inference and reference.

Although what we now know as the "philosophy of language" had not yet sprung full-blown in the Western mind, Kant's reduction of the knowable world to the prior structures of human understanding laid the groundwork

---

[7] See Abrams, *Natural Supernaturalism*.
[8] Matthew Arnold, *Literature and Dogma* (New York: Frederick Ungar, 1970), p. 9.

for the twentieth century vogue of linguistic conventionalism. The Kantian "concepts" became Wittgenstein's "depth grammar." And just as Wittgenstein's language philosophy threw into question the assumption that words represent actual entities, or that meaning can be coupled at all with systems of denotation, so Kant's "Copernican revolution" undercut the notion that "judgements of cognition" could be regarded as forms of rational insight in the older sense of the term. As Kant pointed out in the opening of his first Critique, the claims of reason had to be justified or "deduced" by appeal to the peculiar configurations of thought itself. In short, the theory of knowledge was subtly redrafted as the theory of interpretation. The slurring of the distinction between epistemology and hermeneutics may indeed have been the basis for the ascendancy of the philosophy of history in the nineteenth century. As Hayden White notes, the philosopher of history endeavored not merely to comprehend the meaning of historical affairs, but to execute as well the criteriology for speaking of history as "meaningful." Philosophy of history was really an epistemology of human events. Thus, according to White, it was no more happenstance that philosophy of language had its beginnings among such pioneering philosophers of history as Hegel and Nietzsche.[9]

The habit of viewing history as the matrix of the theory of knowledge, conceived anew as the problem of interpretation, brought into full clarity, however, the dilemma of relativism. In classical epistemology the accession to relativism was but a greedy temptation, draped philosophically as skepticism. It ensued naturally as a dialectical possibility of self-reflection and as part of the critique of authority, as Descartes had demonstrated in the opening of his *Meditations*. But it did not belong to the essential features of the given subject matter. The meteoric growth of "historical consciousness" in the nineteenth century, on the other hand, made the challenge of relativism an indefeasible portion of philosophical hermeneutics. Neo-Kantianism, which prevailed throughout the historicist camp, routinely sought to dissolve relativism by positing some kind of superhistorical principle of understanding. Even Nietzsche with his doctrine of the "will to power" slipped into this bad habit. What appeared as the central element of the relativist muddle was a proliferation of symbols and the multiplicity of texts. As late as the Napoleonic era the "problem" of the text as text had not yet emerged. The reason was quite evident: only Scripture, as the compendium of God's intention and dealings, posed a serious problem of interpretation. Outside the realm of Biblical theology the issue was not so much one of how to mediate the inscriptions of the past, but which authority to accept. Throughout the seventeenth and eighteenth century the debate was between so-called "ancients" and "moderns", and it turned on the question of

---

[9] Hayden White, *Metahistory: The Historical Imagination in Nineteenth-Century Europe* (Baltimore, MD: The Johns Hopkins Press, 1973), p. 428.

which body of literature, or philosophical temperment, one should gravitate toward.

In many respects Nietzsche may be considered the first modern thinker to consider the problem of the text, which is itself the chief hermeneutical conundrum, as something other than a matter of authority, or authorship. For Nietzsche, the written word by its very nature dissembles. Nietzsche anticipated psychoanalysis rather astutely with his special modification of the theory of ideology, which had already been developed. It was Nietzsche who made it known that language must inherently lie, and that the lie is an effect of the embedding of linguistic form within the dynamics of "life." Nietzsche understood language itself as the primary instrument in the genesis of self-deception, which is intimately coupled with the rise of "consciousness." According to Nietzsche, "the world of which we can become conscious is only a surface- and sign-world."[10] This sign-world of consciousness masks an ontology that is inaccessible to articulate speech. Nietzsche identified such an ontology with what is biologically primitive, with the "animal" and instinctual. Its meanings and emblems can only be deciphered by reverse extrapolation, as when one reads a message in a mirror. After Nietzsche the neo-Kantian effort to construct some kind of historical metalanguage, a Rosetta stone for all texts, became increasingly futile. Wrote Nietzsche: "this has given me the greatest trouble and still does: to realize that what things are called is incomparably more important than what they are."[11] In fine, the play of signs in the universe of human discourse became a honeycomb of disassembled intentions, a fissioned teleology that could never be reconstructed except in the endless disporting of interpretation. With Nietzsche the text itself, rather than that of which the text supposedly speaks, becomes the aim of interpretation. The text now constitutes a system of dislocations which provides hints, but no instants of reference; it points to what is lost or vanished, not what is present. The mode of theological thinking that guides interpretation is an imagining of God's "death." But what is signified by this death is not the impossibility of the theological quest, as Nietzsche's metaphor has been wrongly construed, but its relocation. The angle of theological vision is now toward the forgotten and archaic, toward the "word" as aboriginal schema, as pre-utterance.

The pre-utterance, however, as the proper subject of a bathotheology, which amounts to theological thinking *de profundis*, can only be interpreted or "explicated" in the classic sense to the degree that it is absolved of all formality, that it is revealed ineluctably by what now stands in its place and by the same token bars all return to pristine beginnings. The pre-utterance in its fantasized eternity can only be shown at the scene of its repression and

---

[10] Friedrich Nietzsche, *The Gay Science*, trans. Walter Kaufman (New York: Random House, 1974), p. 299.

[11] *The Gay Science*, p. 121.

by virtue of the subterfuge of written text themselves, which belong to what Paul de Man has termed "the rhetoric of temporality." It discourse is the confession of grief and loss. The Nietzschean "annunciation" of the divine demise, when grasped in this most radical context, points not to a contemporary moment, as the so-called "death of God" theologians were wont to claim, but to the changeover in the ancient temple of religious truth from an apprehension of meaning as unmediated force to the consecration of language—the new Deity, figuratively speaking. How else are we to make sense out of Nietzsche's parable of the madman in which the proclamation of God's death is seen as a distant event that has taken "light years" to reach the ears of humankind? Or that God's murderers, who are strangely not aware of the consequence of their own deed, are charged with "drinking up the sea"—the transformation of the watery abyss of what is unsaid into the "saying" of the creation text, the great *let there be* that establishes the world through a recorded utterance.[12]

Theological thinking requires interpretation, because interpretation has its beginnings in the tangled logic of what has been coded in historical obscurity. According to Paul Ricoeur, the very task of interpretation is akin to the Freudian dream-work; it operates by "dissimulating its object under a substituted object." For that reason Freudian psychology, or psychoanalysis, "knows only 'translations' of texts, different versions which come from no original text."[13] The dissimulation of text upon text casts a shadow backwards to the primordial saying, which strangely enjoys no semantic privilege or canonical originality, because it has been effaced in its very entry into the theater of meaning; its birth is its death. Classical theology, as a prehermeneutical system of correspondences between kerygmatic truth and its "application" in the meditation or sermon, was always based on the ancient ideal of authorship—the founding of a tradition through a primal revelation, life work, or moral example. The classical structure of textual validation, therefore, centered upon the metaphysical principle of deduction from first principles, from the semantic rule of derivation from fixed premises as in the logic of the Aristotellian syllogism, or even from the clerical formula of apostolic succession. Heidegger's critique of the "onto-theological" character of Western thought was built on his understanding of how this structure has been elaborated over time as the very grammar of philosophical reasoning. A similar argument is posed by Gadamer in his effort to ground hermeneutics as the science of interpretation in a fundamental reorientation of the view of

12 Consider the following excerpt from Nietzsche's parable of the madman: "The madman jumped into their midst and pierced them with his eyes. 'Whither is God?' he cried; 'I will tell you. We have killed him—you and I. All of us are his murderers? But how did we do this? How could we drink up the sea? Who gave us the sponge to wipe away the entire horizon? What were we doing when we unchained this earth from its sun?" *The Gay Science*, p. 181.

13 Paul Ricoeur, "Psychoanalysis and Art", in Joseph H. Smith (ed.), *Psychiatry and the Humanities* (New Haven, CN: Yale University Press, 1976), p. 21.

language and reality. Language does not refer to, or mirror, an ideal essence
but interpenetrates in a most ambiguous fashion the infinite realm of consciousness. According to Gadamer, even Medieval thinking with its tendency to follow Greek metaphysics and regard the word as intelligible species
failed to grasp "the enigma of its incarnation." Things do not precede their
"manifestation in language," but are part of a universal plenum of possible
significations. Thus "the illusion of the possibility of the universal objectification of everything and anything completely obscures the universality itself."[14] The "logic" of the utterance appears not in the formality of the
statement, but in what the early Heidegger terms its "apophantic" impulse,
its struggle toward manifestation as form and figuration. It is a kind of
dreamwork, insofar as it begets its truthfulness not from the measure of
correspondence, but from the ongoing analogies of interpretation. It is mask
upon mask, disport upon disport, intimation upon intimation.

Theological thinking engages itself with the "dreamwork" of history,
texts, and the cultural imagination not because one should assume, as has
been the fashion in recent years, that these opaque subject areas are somehow preferred to the traditional Christian witness as canonical objects for
consideration. Nor should theological thinking itself take on the camouflage
of a dream, as some enthusiasts for the literature of "deconstruction" have
archly proposed. Theological thinking descends into the hermeneutical laby-
rinth, into the archaic and unmistakably "archaeological", because it is in
that realm that the full meaning of what has remained unsaid or unspoken
concerning the "founding" of the canonical word of incarnation can at last be
flushed from the historical sink of misconstructions. Theological thinking
consists in a recovery project, an attempt to espy and descry not what has
been forgotten, but what was never spoken or thought upon *within the
context of the founding itself*. That is the crucial point of Gadamer's account of
the hermeneutical enterprise overall. "Interpretation," he says, "is not an
occasional additional act subsequent to understanding, but rather understanding is always an interpretation, and hence interpretation is the explicit
form of understanding." Neither a hermeneutical theology, nor a theological
hermeneutics, is what is required of interpretation in the most original
characterization of thinking.[15] What is required is a theological thinking that

[14] Hans-Georg Gadamer, *Philosophical Hermeneutics*, trans. David E. Linge (Berkeley, CA:
University of California Press, 1976), p. 78. Gadamer's linguistics, and therefore his hermeneutical theory, is actually an elevated form of philosophical esthetics. Hermeneutics is, in
fact, "ontological explanation" which follows the trajectory of the "work of art" as self-represen-
tation, the coming into existence of hidden potentialities for meaning through a "transformation
into structure". For "the transformation into a structure means that what existed previously no
longer exists. But also that what now exists, what represents itself in the play of art, is what is
lasting and true." Hans-George Gadamer, *Truth and Method* (New York: Crossroad Publishing,
1982), p. 100.
[15] *Truth and Method*, p. 274.

cannot be distinguished at all from the task of hermeneutical inquiry, because it has no strict canon or method. It purports only to reclaim the lost signatures of divinity, as perhaps Freud sought to exhume the trackings of repressed human will, in the midst of the wilderness of time and memory.

The "pre-text" for such a foray is the Augustinian tradition itself. The distinct starting point of Augustinian thought has always been the quest for the *visio Dei* through analysis of the soul's own constitution and recollections. The framework for the Augustinian "inquest" was, of course, neo-Platonic philosophy with its distinction between sense impressions, as the domain of illusion, and inward reflection as the source of coherent and rational knowledge. True awareness of God is a kind of "recalling," a paleography of the logos itself.". . . in that realm of eternal truth from which all things temporal were made, we behold with our mind's eye the pattern upon which our being is ordered, and which rules all to which we give effect with truth and reason, in ourselves or in the outer world. Thence we conceive a truthful knowledge of things, which we have within us as a kind of word, begotten by an inward speech, and remaining with us after its birth."[16] The whole of Augustine's *Confessions* is this cultivation of the sense of the divine immensity through the articulation of memory, which Augustine describes as "like a great field or spacious place, a storehouse for countless images of all kinds." At a superficial level the Augustinian approach resembles the role of therapy—a purgation or *catharsis* of damaged or distorted motivations within the psyche so that a healthful state can be recaptured. The Platonic ideal of philosophical contemplation was originally therapeutic in its scope. But what singly differentiates the Augustinian outlook from the Platonic is the nature of the object of therapy itself. Both the Platonic and Freudian methods rest on the Greek cosmopsychology, which identifies supreme insight with self-recognition, the contemplation of the highest form or "idea" in the Elysian fields of thought. Augustine, however, sought to penetrate beyond the structure of finite intelligence into the infinite, and in principle unfathomable, reaches of the divine spirit itself. The scrutiny of one's own memory, for Augustine, is not merely therapeutic, but inherently dialectical. Whereas memory in the therapeutic tradition consists chiefly in the repository of the forgotten, in Augustine it is the threshhold of the unseen, the borderland of wisdom. "The power of the memory is prodigious, my God. It is a vast, immeasurable sanctuary. Who can plumb its depths? And yet it is a faculty of my soul. Although it is part of my nature, I cannot understand all that I am. This means, then, that the mind is too narrow to contain itself entirely. But where is the part of it which it does not itself contain? Is it somewhere outside itself and not within it? How, then, can it be part of it, if it is not contained in it?"[17]

16 Augustine, *Later Works*, trans. John Burnaby (Philadelphia: The Westminster Press, 1955), p. 65.

17 Augustine, *Confessions*, trans. R. S. Pine-Coffin (New York: Penguin Books, 1961), p. 216.

The Greeks believed that the therapeutic path restores the mind to its natural equilibrium. The metaphor of tuning a lyre was often utilized to signify the *ordo salutis*, the regimen of both "health" and "salvation." But for Augustine, the archaeology of the psyche discloses that the psyche can never "contain itself entirely." Instead, the therapeutic moment turns out to be an instant of revelation, an encounter with the wholly other.

The Augustinian "insearch," as James Hillman has termed the pursuit of the sacred within the abyss of psychic life, thus represents the central hermeneutical moment within the circuit of theological thinking. But theological thinking, as we have stressed, is not a form of esoteric divination in which somehow secret knowledge, or gnosis, is extracted from the well of collective myth and memory. Theological thinking in its hermeneutical *descensus in infernus* forces its way into what might best be termed the "mirror world" of the imagination, the underside of constructive rationality. That is where the role of depth psychology comes to play in contemporary theological work. The fusion of theology and psychology, which really ensues with Schleiermacher, has been something of troublesome matter for the traditional conservations about "God." If God is *ens realissimum*, the ontological vector of transcendence for all inqury and argumentation, in what sense can either the concept or symbol of divinity be regarded as residing in the interior of self-consciousness. Certainly the investigations and speculations of thinkers such as Jung have tempted us strongly to move in that direction. For the testimony of the client in analytical psychology, especially in a post-dogmatic era when "experience" counts as the touchstone of all truthfulness, seems quite convincing to the theologian. In one respect the fascination of theology nowadays with depth psychology can be looked upon as a revival of the Medieval contemplative tradition, which in turn reflected the monastic preoccupation with the health and destiny of the soul. The Augustinian "word of the heart" manifests itself when the sense of the divine power in nature and history has eroded.

Yet, at the same time, the temptation of "psychologism" in theology should be scrutinized because of the grave possibility of confusing the real with what is in "error." Freudian psychoanalysis has its beginnings in the hermeneutics of the "erroneous." As Freud himself proclaimed in his third lecture of his *General Introduction to Psychoanalysis*, "accumulated and combined errors are certainly the finest flowers of the species. If we were only concerned to prove that errors had a meaning, we should have limited ourselves to them at the outset, for the meaning in them in unmistakable, even to the dullest intelligence, and strong enough to impress the most critical judgement."[18] The Freudian "psychology of error," or the attempt to catalogue and chart a "psychopathology" of the ordinary and mundane,

---

[18] Sigmund Freud, *A General introduction to Psychoanalysis*, trans. Joan Riviere (New York: Washington Square Press, 1961), p. 69.

comprised the very foundation of the analytic methodology. In that respect it may be construed as its organon for exegesis, as the very leverage of interpretation for the building up of what would later be known as Freud's metapsychology. The Freudian search for archaic instinctual patterns, for codes and ciphers that reveal both the prehistory and the racial determinants of the "civilized" mind, evolved straightaway and with crisp logic out of the fundamental insights gained with the examination of the meaning of "error." The importance of error, for Freud, is that it represents a kind of unknown knowledge, a speaking of the unspoken, an occult discernment whose revelatory capacity is its very lack of intelligibility. With regard to dreams, Freud notes: "In the first place, we are confronted with the fact that the dreamer has at his command a symbolic mode of expression of which he knows nothing, and does not even recognize, in his waking life. This is as amazing as if you made the discovery that your housemaid understood Sanscrit, though you know that she was born in a Bohemian village and had never learnt that language."[19] The automatism of dream imagery derives from a strange outworking of what Freud dubbed the "excitation" of the unconscious. The rationality of the dream transaction hides an embedded, libidinous "logic" that is based on the devious expression of repressed contents. It is the same as in slips of the tongue, or other inadvertent "substitutions" in the conscious distribution of discourse. The reference of the linguistic signifier is what remains absent to language. Its epiphany is, in actuality, both a transgression and an inversion. The inversion consists in the replacement of force by meaning, though the latter term bears no structural relation to the former. At the semantic level the inversion is exhibited as a displacement of an ordinary word usage by an inappropriate, and sometimes amusing, counter. As for the "intention" of the displacement, we can say that it is an absolute leap from absence to presence. In a peculiar sense it is a self-creation ex nihilo. The "error" is an act of vagrancy, an intrusion into a realm where it is not expected. Freud himself used the analogy of the unwanted visitor. In certain instances the error engenders the feeling of the "uncanny", which Freud believed constituted the marker of extreme repression, as in the ambivalence experienced toward the deceased.[20] The hermeneutics of repression from the pure semiological standpoint takes us behind the surface grammars of our language and shows us how our very linguisticality is not constitutive, as the Kantian tradition holds, so much as it is a vital form of dissemblance. The dissemblance, of course, is what makes the hermeneutical undertaking both

---

[19] *General Introduction to Psychoanalysis*, p. 173.

[20] "Most likely our fear still contains the old belief that the deceased becomes the enemy of his survivor and wants to carry him off to share his new life with him. Considering our unchanged attitude toward death, we might rather inquire what has become of the repression, that necessary condition for enabling a primitive feeling to recur in the shape of an uncanny effect." Sigmund Freud, *On Creativity and the Unconscious* (New York: Harper & Row, 1958), p. 150.

possible and necessary in the first place. But there is also a profound theological point that can be underscored as well in this connection. The theory of language as dissemblance arouses once again the classical notion of time and space as the estuary containing God's footprints or traces, the view that revelation is progressive through the realization of what heretofore were but "figurations" of an eventual, divine *parousia* or fullness. The dissemblance is what renders impossible the semiological project of a self-contained sign system. It undercuts all reductionist canons and serves as the ground of theological thinking in its most basic modality.

The hermeneutical foundations of all theological thinking, therefore, are integral to the theological enterprise itself, not merely because theological speech and writing demands interpretation, but because language by itself is an "error." The error, in turn, leads us to wander amid the silent citadels of the holy, which is our conventional universe of signifiers. If our thinking necessarily includes the moment of bathotheological peering into the obscurity of what is prelinguistic, of the "going under" of Nietzsche's Zarathustra, then theological thinking per se can never rest content with the exposition of doctrine, or bare apologetics. Theological thinking can never be assimilated principally to psychological thinking, but the psychological dimension in the same breath cannot be ignored, because it is where the unthought—that less tendentious synonym for the repressed—occurs. Before, however, we follow through with what we are suggested here, we must consider the peculiarities of theological language itself.

CHAPTER 9

THEOLOGICAL LANGUAGE, DECONSTRUCTION, AND THE "MARGINALITY" OR DISCOURSE

". . . 'everyday language' is not innocent or neutral. It is the language of Western metaphysics, and it carries with it not only a considerable number of presuppositions of all types, but also presuppositions inseparable from metaphysics, which, although little attended to, are knotted into a system."
— JACQUES DERRIDA

"For the true formula of atheism not *God is dead* . . . the true formula is *God is unconscious*."
— JACQUES LACAN

The increasing interest among members of the theological profession in the French movement known as "deconstruction" has caught many by surprise. The compatibility of an erstwhile Christian and foundationalist theological heritage with what is frequently perceived as an inscrutable and *outre* sect of twentieth century Gallic scholasticism has baffled conventional observers. Such bafflement, however, may be more germane to the form and not the content of deconstructionism's philosophical "dialect". For we find within the donconstructionist idiom a profound iconoclasm which resists in the strongest prophetic sense the imperialism of all linguistic codes and systems.

On that score what is generally known as the "moment of deconstruction"—the point at which the grammatical token, the signifier, the vehicle of reference, discloses itself as void of all ontological gravity—corresponds in the theological orbit of thinking to a smashing of the idols, which embody pious assurance and doctrinal certainty.[1] We may draw attention, again, to the older Barthian standpoint of "Krisis," which functions as a *mot d'enigme* for the radical incommensurability between theological assertions and the divine eminence. In his later years Barth referred to this paradoxical dimension of theological thinking as the *intellectus fidei*. The mind of faith, says Barth, "is engaged in gathering, although it abstains from equalizing, stereotyping, or identifying. While it gives every point of the circumference its

---

[1] See *Deconstruction and Theology*.

special due, it brings together all parts from their own individual centers to their common center. Theology finds itself committed, freed, and summoned to such knowledge. In the theological act of knowledge, seeing is doubtless an attentive and exact gaze toward one or another special form of the object; as such, it is also sight that views one form together with the others. What is decisive is that it is an insight into the one object which presents itself now in this, now in that, form, or an insight into one peculiar form which has become a form of the one object."[2] The Barthian "ingathering" of insights and outlooks into the unity of the *intellectus fidei* has a close affinity with what we have described earlier as the all-embracing penetration of theological thinking into the domains of science, history, and culture. From an older, dogmatic standpoint the rationale for such a band width granted to theology can be summarized as follows: the living God is Lord of all seasons and places, of all projects and ventures that somehow conspire for his glorification and purpose. Therefore, the mind of faith, not to mention the depths of theological thinking itself, must encompass far more than what is its narrow and appropriate "subject matter." The false representations of Deity, the spurious, "little gods", must melt away before the theological gaze, because in their finite pretension to infinite majesty they work to close off the authentic unity of all symbols and modes of veneration under the aspect of supreme revelation. That is why so-called "natural theology" must always be construed as a dangerous interloper from the Barthian perspective. For the natural standpoint of religious consciousness mistakes the plurality of mythic archetypes, ciphers, and proximal images for the oneness of the One who is always wholly other. The distinction reaches back to Paul's Letter to the Romans.[3] Hence, the iconoclastic imperative within what Barth called "evangelical theology" has a similar, self-critical, "theoretical" basis within deconstructionism's campaign against the metaphysics of the given.

But "deconstruction" first and foremost constitutes a critique of the philosophy of language; and it is in the domain of linguistic analysis that the full force of Derrida, who placed the word in general circulation, can be felt. Derrida's identification of the "moment" of deconstruction arose from his deliberations on the problems of Husserlian phenomenology, particularly the recognition that linguistic meaning or "representation" demands that one

[2] Karl Barth, *Evangelical Theology: An Introduction* (Grand Rapids, MI: William B. Eerdmans, 1963), p. 88.

[3] See Romans 1:19–23, NEB. "For all that may be known of God by men lies plain before their eyes; indeed God himself has disclosed it to them. His invisible attributes, that is to say his everlasting power and deity, have been visible, ever since the world began, to the eye of reason, in the things he has made . . . knowing God, they have refused to honour him as God, or to render him thanks. Hence all their thinking has ended in futility, and their misguided minds are plunged in darkness. They boast of their wisdom, but they have made fools of themselves, exchanging the splendour of immortal God for an image shaped like mortal man . . ."

abstract from the pure presencing of the life world.[4] This ontological discovery became the basis of a powerful revision in the theory of signification. For the classic theory of signs, derived on the main from the correspondence model of truth, has always assumed that the act of semantic indication pivots upon some king of linkage between a transient reference and an eternal referent. The stance of deconstruction requires that the eternal referent—the ideal of "presence"—be abandoned as a metaphysical chimera. What language delineates is not a queue of present indications, but a trail of vanishing suggestions, what Derrida calls "traces." The trace is not a signature, but an erasure. Its theological content is always negative. As Derrida notes: "Presence . . . far from being, as is commonly thought, *what* the sign signifies, what a trace refers to, presence, then, is the trace of the trace, the trace of the erasure of the trace. Such is, for us, the text of metaphysics, and such is, for us, the language which we speak."[5] The trace, as opposed to the bare object of signification, belongs completely to time and remains a purely temporal phenomenon. By the same token, it cannot be said to exist within time, insofar as it operates pre-eminently as the vehicle of temporal transition.

A point that should be emphasized here, however, is that Derrida's notion of the trace hinges largely on the privileged status which he bestows upon *writing*. Hence, all ontological analysis must be comprehended as "grammatology"—the science of inscriptions. Writing, for Derrida, is the proper subject matter for philosophical consideration, because it consists in the primal movement of expression from the presence of voice (what Derrida terms the *phoneme*) to the re-presentation of the "grammatical", that is, the written, formality (i.e., the *grapheme*). The written formality engenders not a true signification but a trace, because what it betokens has already been left behind and covered over. The original word is never contained within writing, even though writing is what gives words their power to convey and to endure. Writing, therefore, cannot be responsible for an event of *denotation*. On the contrary, its method is exclusively one of "dissemination", the exile of meaning within the kingdom of the text, while the paradise of unmediated presence remains an aging nostalgia for philosophy, an unrequited mythic longing. Traditional textual interpretation endeavors to find a system of correlates beneath the web of signifiers akin to what Wittgenstein dubbed a "depth grammar." It strives after what Derrida calls the "tutelary meaning." Classic modes of interpretation have their own unique teleology, which are also "totalizing." Yet the process of dissemination, which lies at the heart of deconstruction, "although producing a nonfinite number of semantic

---

[4] See Jacques Derrida, *Speech and Phenomena and Other Essays on Husserl's Theory of Signs* (Evanston, IL: Northwestern University Press, 1973), p. 48ff.

[5] Jacques Derrida, *MARGINS of Philosophy*, trans. Alan Bass (Chicago: University of Chicago Press, 1982), p. 66.

effects, can be led back neither to a present of simple origin . . . nor to an eschatological presence. It marks an irreducible and *generative* multiplicity."[6]

On first reading the theological appropriation of Derrida can lead to a half-critical nihilism, which repudiates the very coherence not just of value-statements, but also of so-called theological utterances—the kind that seek to ground and anchor all finite locutions of grammars in a representation of the ultimate. Indeed, Derrida himself contends the movement of deconstruction, which overcomes all forms of idealism or "logocentrisms", leads to an erasure not merely of immediate presence, but of eternal presence as well. The reign of writing is simultaneously the deconstitution of all religious symbolics. It underscores the end of theology to the extent that it exposes the emptiness of the God-cipher, the so-called "transcendental signified." God "died," for Derrida, not at Calvary, as writers such as Altizer in the past have maintained, but during Moses' descent from Sinai. The instant the all-consummating divine epiphany, first incarnate in speech with the self-disclosure of the unnameable name from out of the burning bush, is transformed into what Derrida terms the "supplement" of language, the awesome timelessness of holy presence becomes radically temporal, and thereby finite. The vast *logos* of Creation is constricted, scarred, "graphed" within the tablets. The presencing of the Present One, strangely but indefeasibly, now manifests itself as the stony authority of the Law.

If one simply adopts the radical criticism of semantico-metaphysics implicit in standard philosophy of language, the outcome is bound to be close to what Mark Taylor dubs an "a/theology."[7] The trajectory of Derridaean reflection leads to a reverse ontology. Such a codification represents an honest reckoning of where modern theology all along has been gravitating. A metaphysics of the void, as Nietzsche wryly commented, is but a palliative for the final, roughshod embrace of the world's underlying purposelessness.[8] An "a/theology" counts as an eschatological wince, a holding fast through the reifying power of discourse itself of the moment of deconstruction. However, from Nietzsche's standpoint the truth of all formally concocted a/theologies is a fathomless *a/teleology*, which best describes the message behind the wan hieroglyphs of language.

So-called "deconstruction" can never become a new hermeneutical foundation of theological work, in the same manner that such sundry philosophical fashions as Aristotelianism, common-sense empiricism, Romantic

[6] Jacques Derrida, *Positions*, trans. Alan Bass (Chicago: University of Chicago Press, 1981), p. 45.

[7] See Mark Taylor, *Erring: A Postmodern A/theology* (Chicago: The University of Chicago Press, 1984).

[8] Consider Nietzsche's concluding rhetoric in *The Genealogy of Morals:* "Man would sooner have the void for his purpose than be void of purpose . . ." *The Birth of Tragedy and the Genealogy of Morals*, trans. Francis Golffing (Garden City, NY: Doubleday, 1956), p. 299.

idealism, and of course existentialism have served as forms of apologetic leverage in their own heydays. The logic of the deconstructive "critique" patently aims to strip away all philosophical baselines, exposing their discrete metaphysical environments. Deconstruction can never give theology another "post-modern" context of language from which it might somehow speak profoundly and meaningfully. Deconstruction by its own self-admission brings about a cataclysm of syntax. It rends irreversibly the veil of the temple of reference. It forces all theological language, and by extension theological thinking as well, to the furthest margins of discourse, where words no longer "connote" in a customary and casual sense, where venerable systems of signs and associations blur into phantasmagoria of unvoiced inklings.

From the side of both metaphysics and semiotic theory the skewing of language itself toward the "unthought" dusk of the margins may be perceived as a dangerous tendency, as a prospective transgression against the sovereignty of grammar. Indeed, the direct theological adaptation of deconstruction's moment of "difference," in which the presence of the present as laid bare in language's web of representations is tragically experienced as loss, as "nothingness", as absence, must for all time ensue in a vision of nihilism. The nihilism of theology and philosophy, as Heidegger has pointed out, arises from their long-standing dogmatic propensities. Because both theology and philosophy seek to posit objects of knowledge by methods of exposition, demonstration, and argumentation, the disclosure that the object has been evacuated by the flux of discourse, that it has been "deconstructed," that it has sublimed into the "trace", emulates the horror of an empty cosmos. So much of traditional theology, therefore, is a grand and silent mausoleum in which can be heard the withdrawing footfalls of ancient signs. From the side of theological thinking, which does not grudge to confront the abyss, the exile of language to the margins of meaningfulness discloses a passage beyond the finitude of all linguistic representations themselves. At this very gateway between the familiar and the strange, between the evidentiary and the ineffable, between presence and transcendence, the *moment* of deconstruction transpires. The moment is not one to be dwelt upon and remembered, for it cannot be inscribed in discourse. Like the clanging of an abbey bell at vespers, the moment of deconstruction announces the arrival of the holy. And by the "holy" we mean simply the presence that is concurrently present and absent, that is not a mystical obliteration of the various contradictions of experience, but their full expression.

Since the recent "appropriation" of deconstruction, chiefly by Protestant theologians infected with its iconoclastic fervor, there has been a trend toward reducing theological issues to literary or rhetorical matters. The sportive and opaque tenor of so-called "post-critical" narratives, particularly in the case of Derrida's later essays, has been strongly conducive to this set of circumstances. Philosophical writing has been turned into a harlequinade, an interminable word-circus within the body of the text, so that the deconstructive "principle" slips from view. The situation can readily be compared to the declining years of linguistic analysis, when the Wittgensteinian rule of "showing" the meaning of a term through its contextual application rapidly degenerated into a rococo kind of expository style thoroughly mindless of the premises and "problems" of the philosophical world. Yet deconstruction in its root uses can be taken up as a powerful, critical tool. If in a very simplistic and elegant sense we mean by "deconstruction" the commitment of both philosophical method and theological insight to portraying the limits of all reifying modes of communication, thereby underscoring that language is not a "mirror of nature," as Richard Rorty would say,[9] but a self-enfolded universe of indices, intimations, and allusions, then the summons to theological thinking becomes apparent. The marginality of theological discourse—i.e., its own self-distancing from "everyday" language and phenomena—is embedded within a radical, new understanding of what language in its generic guise actually amounts to. Theological utterances are not a separate species of utterances overall, but an internal confession, a *cri de coeur*, of all speakers who recognize from whence their uncanny capacity for language itself comes. Theological thinking is not, as it might be construed on metaphysical grounds, a peculiar passion of thinking on the whole, but the reflection of thought itself back to its primeval, abyssmal, and "unthought" beginnings. Certainly this notion that language is not conventional, but archival, enthustiastically drove the researches of early modern linguistics, which in turn started from the Romantic presupposition that there must be a profound continuity between contemporary dialects and a forgotten *Ursprache*, an original, purely poetic argot. The Romantic tendency to historicize semantic and categoreal relations, as exhibited in their fascination with different evolutionist theories, concealed what was perhaps their own half-conscious discovery of the bathotheological principle, the realization that reality is not hard-edged, but a winding stair of deep-layered connections and affinities. The Romantic hermeneutical touchstone that eternity is not segregated from, but interlaced with time, offered a metaphysical way of stating what we would now call the "deconstructive" attitude—in essence, that "things" are not proxies for terms, but spectral correlates of the language process in which the solidity of the written text displaces the phonetic present, in which meaning emerges from the fragmenting of the lattice of conventional signifiers.

The relation of the emerging deconstructive attitude in contemporary letters to the more pedigreed philosophy of language is becoming slowly apparent. What has not been recognized, on the other hand, is the intimate affiliation between deconstruction and the effort to plumb the "psychic"

---

[9] See Richard Rorty, *Philosophy and the Mirror of Nature* (Princeton, NJ: Princeton University Press, 1978).

penumbra of discourse. The relationship is important, because long before Derrida ever contoured his critical rule that signs do not really "signify", but constitute a moment of effacement, the deconstructive attitude was already present in the "archaeological" work of Freud. The tradition of French linguistics ostensibly makes Derrida a renegade pupil of Ferdinand Saussure, yet deconstructive heuristics are more profoundly rooted in the clinical methodology of psychoanalysis. Consider the following description of the "sign", the essential medium of "semiotics", tendered by Derrida in his homage to the French *philosophe* Condillac: "Signs classify and enlighten. Are they, for all that, without force? There is also a force, a quantity of the analogy of signs. And we must ask ourselves what relation there is between practical force and the theoretical force which comes in short to *remark* how the confused ideas regulating our actions, how prelinguistic and presemiotic judgements and mute analysis 'make us act'. For there is idea, judgement, and analysis before all signification. By signification, we must understand activity, activation itself, activation putting into an articulatable chain, signification as concatenation, concatenation as distinction. Before signification, sensation analyzes, judges, knows, but in confusion and obscurity, say in the natural light of instinct."[10]

Since the advent of psychoanalysis, the question has abided: to what extent is that abyssmal font of pre-linguistic force (Freud's "unconscious", Derrida's "natural light of instinct") intelligible as discourse? Freud puzzled over this matter for most of his life, and wound up utilizing broken myths and relatively crude metaphysical, or "metapsychological", constructions to contend with the enigma. For Freud, Oedipus was not merely a didactic image; the myth aimed to energize and embody, as *Christos* did for Paul, the most fundamental and soul-wrenching tensions of human conception and experience. The tortured ambivalence of an erotic fascination with mother and a murderous rage against the paternal served for Freud as the very axis of modernity within its own symbolic reserves. Only the myth (or should we say the "bathomythical" schema?) suffices as the true totality of appropriate discourse. But this substitution of the mytheme for the phoneme, the archetype for the text, rests upon the impossibility of discourse as a nexus of signifiers penetrating beyond the stock logic of subject and predicate, of "raising" the instinctual contents of the unconscious into the luminosity of the word. The dredging up of psychic force and clarifying it as speech has always been the formidable task of analysis. In the words of Jacques Lacan: "One began only to repeat after Freud the word of his discovery: *it speaks*, and, no doubt, where it is least expected, namely, where there is pain."[11] In the semiotic world "it" is incapable of speaking. Discourse seeps from the

[10] Jacques Derrida, *The Archaeology of the Frivolous: Reading Condillac*, trans. John P. Leavey, Jr. (Pittsburgh: Duquesne University Press, 1980), p. 197.

[11] Jacques Lacan, *Écrits: A Selection*, trans. Alan Sheridan (New York: W.W. Norton, 1977), p. 125.

metaphysical stratum of words in their denotations and relations. The subject of discourse if the speaker who reflects back upon what he has seen, touched, or heard. Yet at the very margins of meaning this structure of correlations breaks down. The "subject" of discourse is something divorced from its unfoldment. The signification is dislodged from its intention.

Freud first encountered this phenomenon in dreams and mistaken utterances, slips of the tongue, or what he termed "parapraxes." The casual remark or the dream representation appear as a riddle that must be deciphered. The contriving of a riddle by the "unconscious" results from its hiding from the subject of the authentic *subject matter*, which would generate unmanageable pain were it to surface. But why is a riddle produced in the first place? One of the strangest aporias in Freudian thought come out of the disjunction between the ordinary testament of the patient and the peculiar, sometimes even "uncanny", form of the interpretation. The so-called "hermeneutics of suspicion" employed by psychoanalysis necessitates that the manifest level of discourse be almost automatically collapsed into its depth counterpart, which is obfuscated or "latent." The concrete discourse of the patient is taken as a mask of what is essentially beyond discourse, and what must be brought to presence by some kind of hermeneutical extortion.

The extortion, however, does not disclose the real element of the unconscious, only the distorted wish which comes to be rectified in the flitting light of therapy. Thus, if one inspects the Freudian "metaphysics" in all its subtlety and rococo majesty, one finds a fundamental, philosophical problem that dogged Kant and was ultimately resolved through the Hegelian dialectic. It is the well-known epistemological question of the "thing in itself." The thing in itself, for Kant, was a limit rather than an entity. As numerous philosophical commentators on Kant have stressed, the thing in itself served as a monument to the final boundaries of both perception and discourse. Freudian conceptions such as the "repressed" or the "unconscious desire" function in much the same manner. Because Freud was committed to various metaphysical schemas, with such designations as "topographical" or "hydraulic", used to elaborate clinical data, he never sought to unwind the complicated discursive dilemmas of the psychoanalytic enterprise himself. Had Freud, or any of his immediate followers bearded that challenge, the analytical adventure of interpretation might in time have coalesced as the bedrock of a new "psychic silence."

A psychic science, as opposed to an idiosyncratic kind of gnosis, was not the destiny of Freudian thinking, primarily because the rather tendentious notion of a the unconscious having a "logic" never became part of a general psycho-semantics. The semantic properties of Freudian psychopathology, together with the discourse of therapeutic intervention, have never been dissected in any rigorous or systematic manner with the tools of philosophy, although restricted forays have been attempted here and there. Yet the reappropriation of psychoanalysis itself as a semantic system can be found in the work of Lacan. For Lacan, the unconscious is not a mysterious region of the psyche, but "that part of the concrete discourse, in so far as it is transindividual, that is not at the disposal of the subject in re-establishing the continuity of his conscious discourse."[12] The unconscious is a text, "that chapter of my history that is marked by a blank or occupied by a falsehood: it is the censored chapter."[13] Symptoms are not indicators, but grammars all their own. Indeed, they are *symbols,* although they fall within a grammatology all their own. According to Lacan, the dream takes the guise of a "sentence," a rebus; "it has the structure of a form of writing."[14] Its "sententious" nature arises from the fact that it is an embedded type of discourse that seeks to be liberated from its own vein. Dream logic is a "paralogic," but it is not a logic all its own; it stems from the distortion of subjective discourse to the extent that the subject is lost entirely, i.e., *dissociated.* In Lacan's words, the language of the unconscious is the "discourse of the other."

Freud's "discovery" of the unconscious was not something epochal and without precedent, according to Lacan. What touched off Freud's revolution was his recognition that the unconscious is not a primordial given—which was later repudiated by the Jungians—but a kind of lacuna, a "cut" created by the scission of the ordinary subject from its psychological legacy. The unconscious is wholly a production of the "censor." The negation of desire creates a reserve of unspoken speech, a muzzled capacity for utterance. Because the unconscious betokens this compendium of unthought alterity, it is not, as Freud himself unfortunately intimated through his choice of phraseology, a thing itself, an apophantic specter, a locked and barred midnight castle, but a *grammar* all its own. Thus, Lacan asserts that "the unconscious is structured like a language," and the otherness of its form "is the locus in which is situated the chain of the signifier that governs whatever may be made present of the subject—it is the field of that living being in which the subject has to appear."[15] So much of Western philosophy, and by extension psychology, has been both haunted and daunted by Cartesian subjectivism, in which the self-referencing and self-certifying force of the reflective ego becomes the means by which reality is defined. But the Cartesian habit of realizing the subject through self-reference is shot through with contradictions, Lacan argues. The more the "I" underscores itself as subject, the more it automatically relegates to the sphere of otherness. That is why the notorious Cartesian avowal of the *cogito,* the "I think", inevitably winds up with the demonstration of God, according to Lacan. God as the cipher for infinite alterity is logically required in the measure that the finite

[12] *Écrits,* p. 49.
[13] *Écrits,* p. 50.
[14] *Écrits,* p. 57.
[15] Jacques Lacan, *The Four Fundamental Concepts of Psycho-Analysis,* trans. Alan Sheridan (New York: W.W. Norton, 1977), p. 203.

subject posits itself as the ground of all that happens to be plausible or intelligible. The cogito, as Hegel would discern two centuries later, generates a spurious form of infinity. Ego psychology, almost by its own inner constraints, demands an expansion of the stock of latent contents, a widening and ever abiding tendency toward mystification. The Lacanian notion that the subject itself is always latent, on the other hand, that it is a "network of signifiers" which must be interpreted out of obscurity, that its alienation from the field of discourse must be transcendend, resolves this insoluble confusion of Cartesian metaphysics. The phenomenon of psychosis will always remain a surd so long as the goal of psychology is the "purification" of the subject. The psychotic dilemma lingers, so long as the analyst fails to see that the hallucinatory material of the analysand is but a moment of otherness, for which a proper semantic form has not yet coalesced. Cartesian psychology affirms the necessity of a Gòd, who paradoxically has "nothing to do."[16]

Such a God is otiose, because he has been introjected, lost, censored from the orthodox text of the subject. With the advent of Cartesian metaphysics, God becomes unconscious, that is, wholly other. God vanishes beyond the margins of discourse. Yet the "I" of the divine presence, just like the "I" of the nominal subject, must remain a possibility for both language and thought. Indeed, as Lacan points out, in the Freudian hermeneutic the dream symbol is not an irrational cleft, but a deep, complex, and unbounded—that is, an "overdetermined"—*thought*. It is the thought that is still unthought, that has not been shepherded into conversation. Lacan identifies as the fundamental starting point of the analytic enterprise the well-known Freudian maxim, *Wo es war, soll Ich werden* ("where id was, there shall ego be"). "*Where it was*, the *Ich*—the subject, not psychology—the subject must come into existence."[17]

For Lacan as well as Freud the logic of the unconscious can only be deciphered to the degree that discourse mediates between the implicit "thought" enmeshed within the suppressed content and its explicit symbolization revealed through a dream, a jest, or a confession atop the couch. Discourse, therefore, is not merely a secondary effect of the mute "primary processes" of the unconscious; it stands for the construction of unconscious life itself. Unconscious thinking is not only a mirror form of thought; it is the beginning of thinking in its very depth and essence. The Freudian "dream thought" does not register as an eccentricity of thinking. Such thoughts are, by Freud's own account, "a copious store of psychical structures of the highest order, which is characterized by all the signs of normal intellectual functioning, but is nevertheless withdrawn from consciousness till it emerges in distorted form in the dream content."[18] The distortion evident in the

[16] *Four Fundamental Concepts of Psycho-Analysis*, p. 226.
[17] *Four Fundamental Concepts of Psycho-Analysis*, p. 44.
[18] Sigmund Freud, *On Dreams* (New York: W.W. Norton, 1952), p. 114.

oneiric representation arises from the rudimentary incoherence, caused by the act of repression, of the wish itself, which is but proximately fulfilled in the dream. If we transpose Freud's description of the "dream work" out of the idiom of metaphysics, we learn quickly that desire and dream symbol are always correlative with each other, like intention and meaning within the field of semantics. The dream along has no "signifiers"; its intentionality become manifest in the measure that we are able to infer from the vagrant discourse of the subject what has originally been censored, denied, left out. And its meaning, which in retrospect must be interpreted as a distortion, is purely a consequence of a blockage of the primary processes. Dreams hover at the margins of language, and that is why the consummate dreamer is often mistaken for a madman. The dreamer is articulate, but at a "pathological" level.

Dream language is not merely "forgotten language"; it is also language that has not yet condensed as a system of co-ordinate representations. The struggle toward representation in the guise of a compelling, but baffling dream imagery has been the odyssey of modern thinking. We find such a struggle in symbolist poetry, in surrealist art, in the bardic versions of contemporary music. Modern sensibility did not "uncover" the long-immured logic of dream thinking. Beginning with the Romantic poets, it has endeavored to incarnate an unstated logic that could have not have been graphed or detailed at all in the past. The reason for this new trend can be found in the passion of modernity itself. The age of the modern is the epoch of revolt. Within the modern experiment are mobilized all the unspoken and hitherto rejected strata of consciousness, for generations held at a distance by classicism and Christendom alike. In modernity God does not direct from on high, but drives, as Hegel aptly understood, *from below*. Divine reason is not deductively rational, but an unfathomable "cunning" distilled from the farrago of human wishes and ambitions. Providence is a proper interpretation of incipient chaos.

According to Lacan, the true signification of the unconscious drive eventuates out of its "deconstruction" in the act of discourse. Just as language itself, so far as deconstructionist semantics holds, comes to mean what it means by virtue of a serial displacement of terms, so the bare possibility of psychological discourse turns upon the movement from unreflective longing to satisfaction, from absence to presence. And in the same way that the moment of "difference" in the work of deconstruction exposes the illusion of reference by showing how all we ever know of a locution's "meaning" are the semantic traces deposited by the movement of writing, the "deconstruction of the drive" achieved by psychoanalysis unmasks the fiction of the unconscious itself. For a godless era anesthetized to theology and bewitched by the abracadabra of clinical psychology, the unconscious has served as a surrogate absolute; it has become Derrida's "transcendental signified." In Jungian thought particularly the unconscious has emerged as a proxy for the heavenly, as a mythical topography of the sacral. In that connection Jung himself was prophetic: the modern intellect can no more divest itself of religious "otherworldliness" than the organism can cease breathing.

Nonetheless, this "devolution" of theological reflection away from the contemplation of the transcendent to the adoration of the abyssmal has had a far more sweeping and monumental effect than even the most ambivalent partisans of the theological tradition may care to admit. It has transformed the theological task from an Augustininan *fides quaerans intellectum* ("faith seeking understanding") into, at worst, a neo-Romantic style of gnosis and, at best, an aimless inventory of subjective bagatelles. The metaphysical *reductio* of our much revered "divine science" into a loosely co-ordinated philosophical psychology has been the commanding motive behind the "ending" of theology in recent years. Theology in the past has always required an architectonic, a network of first principles, a deductive foundation upon which to build the agora of modern, pluralist sensibilities. Even the fashionable pragmatist and "secularist" theologies of the last generation were unable to withstand this seduction. The more recent efforts to reify the unconscious, which heuristically is equivalent to the return of the repressed in triumphal procession, can be heard perhaps as a final kind of hosannah to the archetypes of the lower mind, to the "dark lords" of the nether consciousness. The mystification of what the poet Wordsworth termed the "underpowers of the soul"—the passage from psychology as critical method to psychology as occultic obsession—constitutes the rest point, the terminal twilight, the grand coda of the metaphysical enterprise as a whole.

Where metaphysics wizens, theological thinking begins to grow. Theological thinking in the ultimate set of circumstances can never be a trope for psychology, for sociology, for anthropology, or even history itself. Yet it penetrates their very subject matter. Theological thinking at its source and sinews amounts to a movement of self-recognition, minus the metaphysical positing of the "Self" itself, at the "depths of spirit. This movement of self-recognition, which accords linguistically with the movement of deconstruction where truth is learned not as an instant of correspondence but as the joyful knowledge of transcendence, of *difference,* approximates the psychoanalytic moment of discovery. The psychoanalytic moment of discovery, however, is not gnosis, but pain. And in the flicker of pain, signifying the long-standing lesion of consciousness (Lacan's "cut", Freud's "repressed"), both the abyss below and the holy pushing in from on high are disclosed as the unthought polarities of thinking in toto. In the grand and "apocalyptic" moment of deconstruction, when language itself is turned topsy-turvy at the margins and the epiphany of darkness takes shape, then theological thinking rises forth. The history of theology has been the history of the metaphysical pretension of fashioning the final word of theological thinking as a stentorian *telestai*—"it is finished." Where theology ends, however, theological thinking must start anew. Its cry at birth is *maranatha.*

CHAPTER 10

DECONSTRUCTION AND PROCESS THOUGHT:
AN EXCURSUS

"We . . . must take for granted that the things that exist by nature
are, either all or some of them, in motion . . ."
—ARISTOTLE, *Physics*

Since the mid-1970s philosophical theology, particularly on this side of
the Atlantic, has been overshadowed by two perspicuous and increasingly
influential schools of interest—process thought and post-critical hermeneutics, or what has conveniently come to be known as "deconstruction".
Process thought, of course, has been established and accepted in Anglo-
American quarters for a far longer period, and unlike its competitor amalga-
mates the native intellectual traditions of Lockean empiricism and Enlightenment idealism. Post-critical hermeneutics, on the other hand, is a
somewhat curious portfolio of post-war experiments in Continental philosophy, which have only made their way overseas by a *force majeur*, blending
the insights of the later Heidegger with French semiotics and so-called
"post-structuralist" literary theory.

The spawning grounds of process thought have been Methodist semi-
naries and those departments identifying themselves with the "Chicago
school" as well as the distinctly "American" practice of philosophy. The
origins of deconstructionism can be found in the alliance forged during the
1960s between philosophy and literary theory, whose standard bearers have
been Jacques Derrida in Europe together with Yale critics such as Paul de
Man and Geoffrey Hartman and former Princeton philosopher Richard
Rorty. Recently it has had a major impact of a group of theologians whose
collective essays first appeared together in the volume *Deconstruction and
Theology*.[1]

On the face of it, process theology and the deconstruction movement
would appear to be strange bedfellows, if not even odder affiliates. But the
fact that both styles of conversation and inquiry have blossomed simultaneously to occupy the vacuum engendered with the eclipse of the older

---

[1] Essays in the volume *Deconstruction and Theology* are by Robert Scharlemann, Thomas J.
J. Altizer, Mark Taylor, Charles Winquist, Max Myers, and myself.

ideologies and orthodoxies should indicate, if only circumstantially, that a shared set on objectives, though not necessarily a common theme, may be descried between the two. It is not our business to "compare" in the routine sense of the word process theology and deconstructionism. But it will be our intent to elucidate the manner in which the two perspectives constitute parallel, even if they do not turn out to be equally effective, responses to the contemporary theological agenda.

The history of ideas a century from now will most likely commemorate a single and signal feature of twentieth century philosophy and theology. It will remember that age as the dissolution of metaphysics and metaphysical habits of reason. It has been A.J. Ayer, founder of logical positivism, and Heidegger, progenitor if not mentor of the deconstructionist critique of language philosophy, who are most usually reckoned as spear carriers of the campaign against metaphysics. But aside from their well-known arguments it is certainly fair to say that the anti-metaphysical momentum has been carried on along a number of philosophical tracks that are not plainly connected to the positivist and Heideggerian programs.

In order to comprehend what is involved in this broad-based trend of dissolving metaphysics, we must first examine what might be designated the "architecture" of metaphysical reasoning itself. In the opening sections of the *Metaphysics* Aristotle characterizes his investigation as the project of first philosophy" or the "science" of "primary being." First philosophy, according to Aristotle, is grounded in the desire of human beings to "acquire knowledge" (*eidanai*). "Knowledge", therefore, is a vision of the formal structure (*eidos*) of everyday experience. For Aristotle, experience is intimately connected with sense impressions which allow us to ascertain "the many differences among things."[2] Philosophical knowledge, on the other hand, associated by Aristotle with "art," seeks "a comprehension of those similarities in light of which the elements of experience manifest as a unified totality."[3] The achievement of this unified totality, the securing of "eidetic" clarity, is the goal of metaphysics. For the "science" (*episteme*) of metaphysics is concerned with "first principles" (*arche*) and "causes" (*aitia*), that is, with unitary components of knowledge. The metaphysician, therefore, is the "master artisan" when it comes to philosophy. As Aristotle writes in Book Gamma "he who has the highest grasp of beings as beings must be able to talk about the fundamental principles of all being, for he is the philosopher."[4]

Physics in Aristotle's view is an account of motion and its causes. Metaphysics on the other hand is concerned with the source of motion which is immobile. The unmoved mover is "eternally unmoved." Its "relation to its

---

[2] Aristotle, *Metaphysics* 980a21.
[3] *Metaphysics* 981a.
[4] *Metaphysics* 1005b.

object is not subject to change."⁵ Therefore, "true being" (*on*) is timeless and motionless. Movement or what we now term "process" takes place only as a transition from one state to another, as the metamorphosis of "substances" or "primary things"). But the source of change itself, Aristotle's God, is anterior to, and independent of, movement. Metaphysics as the science of eternal objects, as pure *theoria*, as the contemplation of what is immutable, atemporal, and indifferent has nothing to do with average experience. Thus the highest form of philosophy within the Western tradition up until the Enlightenment was always devoted to an explanation of what the Greeks knew as *physis*, i.e., "becoming", in terms nonetheless of what is beyond the merely "physical." The *res verae*, the "things in themselves", were always separated from their simple manifestation. The bifurcation of modern philosophy into a deductive rationalism based squarely on mathematics and a logical atomism alleged describing the structure of sensory input was but a codifying of the ancient Greek dilemma over whether ultimate reality consisted of the evident or the not-so-evident, the immanent or the transcendental, the familiar or the remote, the shifting or the stable. Process, like the infinite, seemed a bit spurious to the Hellenic mind. Hence what has come to be termed "classical theism" in the vocabulary of process thinkers was really a Christianized Aristotelianism that perhaps reached its highwater mark in the dogmatism of the sixteenth and seventeenth centuries.

Whitehead's own process model was devised in order to remedy the defects of classical metaphysics within the constraints of metaphysics itself. If one reads *Process and Reality*, for example, one strongly gets the sense that Whitehead is redoing what Aristotle attempted in the *Metaphysics* by a different tack and method. Whereas Aristotle sets about to formulate a science of first principles, Whitehead sketches the task of "speculative philosophy." The latter, says Whitehead, is "the endeavor to frame a coherent, logical, necessary system of general ideas in terms of which every element of our experience can be interpreted."⁶ And whereas Aristotle anchored his metaphysics in the logic of primacy, Whitehead elevated the rule on "coherence" and the principle of "community." As Whitehead put it in an oft-quoted passage, "it is presupposed that no entity can be conceived in complete abstraction from the system of the universe, and that it is the business of speculative philosophy to exhibit this truth."⁷

This Whiteheadian emphasis on extended concreteness attains its center of gravity in the process conception of the Deity. For unlike "classical theism," process theology holds to a God whose eternity does not conflict with his involvement in time. God participates in the "extensive continuum" that is the world of temporal events. His very nature is modified by his

⁵ Aristotle, *Physics* 260a.
⁶ Alfred North Whitehead, *Process and Reality* (New York: The Free Press, 1969), p. 5.
⁷ *Process and Reality*, p. 6.

temporal experience, and his own immersion, rather than removal, from the dynamic "system of the universe" guarantees that time and eternity are radically co-mingled and reciprocally implied. This displacement of the traditional categories of change onto the divine essence itself has been expressed in a teasing string of oxymorons by Schubert Ogden over a decade ago. "God, one may say, is absolutely relative. Likewise, the one thing about God which is never-changing, and so in the strictest sense immutable, is that he never ceases to change in his real relations of love with his whole creation. Precisely as eminently temporal, God is also of necessity strictly eternal or everlasting."[8] Ogden, of course, is simply articulating the standard Christian incarnational idea of God which pervades the Johannine literature and has stood in opposition to "classical theism" for nearly two millenia. At one level, therefore, the quarrel of process theologians with the substantialist metaphysics of the West is merely a reiteration of Patristic orthodoxy as it struggled with docetism, monophysitism, monarchianism, etc. On the other hand, the Whiteheadian standpoint is more idiosyncratic and a bit more subtle. Whitehead's own "metaphysical" starting point is summed up in a short sentence he penned in 1937: "the essence of existence lies in the transition from datum to issue."[9]

For the Greek, and we might add every, metaphysical outlook the "datum", the bare actuality, the presence of the thing itself (Aristotle's *tode ti*) has been the measure of the real. Even Aristotle's teleology, which is sometimes mistaken for a process view, was built upon the subordination of motion (*kinesis*) to the realization of the pre-existent *eidos*. Yet in Whitehead the situation is dramatically reversed. The given becomes the occasion not for replication, but for novelty. While Aristotle deems the "actual" logically prior to the "potential" and therefore the incentive for change, Whitehead regards the universe's high store of potentialities—which are "prehended" by actual occasions—as the explanation for creativity and transformation. Process, as distinguished from Aristotelian teleology, is not the class of a discrete class of entities. Rather, the opposite is the case. "Process," declares Whitehead, "is the way by which the universe escapes from the exclusions of inconsistency." Furthermore, "in process the finite possibilities of the universe travel toward their infinitude of realization."[10] It is now temporal succession, paradoxically speaking, that has an "eternal" character. Even God is open-ended and evolves from his primordial to consequent status.

If we investigate Greek metaphysics closely, we uncover a distinct morphology governing both its scientific and its logical endeavors. The

[8] Schubert Ogden, "Toward a New Theism," in Delwin Brown et al., *Process Philosophy and Christian Thought* (Indianapolis, IN: Bobbs-Merrill, 1971), p. 185.
[9] Alfred North Whitehead, *Modes of Thought* (New York: The Free Press, 1966), p. 96.
[10] *Modes of Thought*, p. 54.

structure of metaphysical reasoning parallels that of what Aristotle in the *Topics* terms "dialectical deduction. Dialectic, or deductive argument, throughout the history of Western philosophy has been the linchpin of all metaphysical exposition. Aristotle defines deduction as a line of discussion where when "certain claims are laid down," then "something besides the original things arises of necessity from and through them." Furthermore, the success of the deduction or *demonstratio* rests on the self-evidence of the first principles of premises. Each premise should "command belief in and by itself."[11] The self-certification of the premise in the Aristotelian syllogism corresponds to the *tode ti* of the metaphysical subject. Hence, from the simple structuralist standpoint Graeco-Christian metaphysics ("classical theism") can be construed as the speculative elaboration of predicate logic, according to which:

(i) inference proceeds from the positing of an obvious and independent state of affairs

(ii) rational proof or deduction consists in subsuming the particular under the general, or the immediate under the mediate.

Just as metaphysics begins with the "assumption" of universal, rational knowledge (the science of first principles), so logic commences from statements about which there should be no disputing. The "truth value" of an Aristotelian inference, therefore, depends on the validity of the initial thesis from which all judgements about the consequent are derived.

The "counterlogic" of process thought, however, on which its own alternative metaphysical policies are founded, unrolls from the presupposition that the general is logically prior to the particular, the antecedent to the consequent. Such a counterlogic has been worked out in detail by Hartshorne, who distinguishes between what he calls "a-terms" and "r-terms." Hartshorne's terms are the traditional antecedents or substance-terms of classical logic and metaphysics, for example, "cause," "necessary," "infinite," etc. His r-terms, which express the array of concrete entities and relational predicates, represent the consequents or derivatives, such as "subject," "effect," "contingent," and "finite." From a logical point of view the domain of "truth", for Hartshorne, is the field of r-predicates, which is the complete reversal of the Aristotelian project. So far as metaphysics is concerned "we can find the absolute only in the relative, objects . . . only in subjects, causes only in effects, earlier events only in later, being only in becoming, the eternal only in the temporal, the abstract only in the concrete . . . the infinite only in the finite."[12] Substance is not the starting point of process, but vice-versa. The complex precedes the simple, the subjective

---

[11] *Topics* 100a20.

[12] Charles Hartshorne, *Creative Synthesis and Philosophic Method* (LaSalle, IL: Open Court, 1970), p. 119.

aim the objective achievement. "God now" oversees the "God en arche. In summary, process logic rests on this commitment: "in the beginning was [only] the transition."

Aristotelian logic is built on the principle of exclusion, or of non-contradiction. Process logic, in contrast, is anchored in the notion of universal inclusion, or the continuum of contrasts. Inclassical theism God is a personal agency separate from his effects. In process thought God is, according to Hartshorne, "universal or ubiquitous." That is why process theologians, particularly John Cobb, lately have taken such an outstanding interest in Oriental philosophy, especially Buddhism. The problem with process thought, on the other hand, is that by designing itself as a counter-metaphysic shaped by the counterlogic of inclusive opposition, it flouts the rules of metaphysics in the same breath it seeks to rehabilitate them. For that reason many philosophers not steeped in the process idiom find it honeycombed with opaque expressions, unwieldly abstractions, and conceptual muddles. Process theology is in many ways the Alice's looking glass of Western metaphysical theism. And like any looking glass it can only furnish inverted images, not genuine critical breakthroughs.

Unlike Whitehead and his successors, Heidegger recognized that the difficulty with classical metaphysics resides not in its devaluing of temporality, but in the metaphysical pretension itself. Process thought seeks to contend with the deficiencies of metaphysical theism by standing it on its head. Heidegger has undertaken to abolish metaphysics entirely. Process theology has challenged traditional metaphysical thinking on the grounds that it has its categories backwards, that its logic is topsy-turvy. Heidegger and the deconstructionists contend that "truth" is not a property of any system of logical connectives, whether we are treating of parts or of wholes. Truth is contained not in the predicative, but in the manifestation of the prepredicative, not in the thinking of the proper thoughts, but in "thinking the unthought," not in what is said about God, but in the saying of the unsaid.

There is, of course, a tantalizing suggestion here of the accent in process thought on both relation and transition as contrasted with the quiddity of the metaphysical entity. But what distinguishes deconstruction is its concern with the transitions or "movement" of signification in language. Process theology is embedded in nineteenth century metaphysical idealism to the degree that it has ignored what might be described as the "heuristic" or second-order preoccupation of twentieth century philosophy with grammar, semantics, and the functions of discourse. Deconstruction, by comparison, represents the fruition of these hermeneutical instrumentalities, inasmuch as it follows through to the utmost of Heidegger's contention that the "overcoming" of metaphysics must entail a turn to the peculiarities of language itself.

The philosophy of language, according to Derrida who considers even Heidegger's hermeneutical advances far too classical and "logocenteric", is the last stronghold of metaphysics. The metaphysical streak in the philosophy of language is the theory of reference and denotation. The theory of reference, which holds that the meaning of a term or locution is constituted by that which the language "signifies," is based in Derrida's view on the doctrine of the "presence" of the thing mirrored in language. In the same way that metaphysics seeks to elucidate the bare essent, the *tode ti*, the philosophy of language undertakes to disclose as in Husserlian phenomenology (which has always been the touchstone for French linguistics) the pure *eidos*, the "presence of the present" behind the words themselves.

Yet meaning does not reside in the pattern of correspondence between language and object, according to Derrida. It is produced by the moment of "difference." "Difference" is the pivot term in deconstruction as "process" is in process thought; and the semantic valency is well-nigh equivalent. Difference is the hermeneutical "process" whereby meaning is generated in the temporal unfoldment of discourse. Language, particularly written language, exhibits an "order," Derrida argues, "that resists philosophy's founding opposition between the sensible and the intelligible."[13] Once the written character, the grapheme, is posited, it annihilates the linguistic intention, the "presence" of that signified. The presence of the signified, therefore, is revealed only after it is gone, only after it has been dislodged by the movement of language. Presence is shown to be absence, and the signified "object" remains as nought but trace. In fine, "meaning" appears as the difference between the spurious "presence" and the "representation" that is the unit of language. Derrida explains that "with the difference between real presence and presence in representation . . . a whole system of difference involved in language is implied in the same deconstruction: the differences between the represented and the representative in general, the signified and the signifier in general, simple presence and the reproduction . . ."[14] The signified is endlessly *sous rature*, "under erasure." Language is a verb,[15] and it is the verbal force of language that brings forth the "novelty" of the utterance, the saying of the unsaid, the rupture of the linguistic act from the putative phenomenon it "represents." Finally, the philosophy of language is "metaphysical", for Derrida, because it aims toward logical simplicity; it is in quest of what Derrida calls "the transcendental signified," which is the semiological substitute for the "first cause" of metaphysics. Once the metaphysical notion of the transcendental signified as "deconstructed" through the linguistic presentation of difference, then the classical concept of God must follow accordingly, since "speech" about the divine is radically en-

---

[13] *Speech and Phenomena*, p. 133.

[14] *Speech and Phenomena*, p. 52.

[15] The verbal force of language has been conveyed epigramatically in Heidegger's famous dictum *Die Sprache spricht* ("language speaks"). Heidegger, however, was trying in this expression, as in others, to show ostensivebly how language "means" through the process of speech itself.

twined with the reality of the divine itself. Derrida's grounding of semantics in process, rather than in Greek noetics which distinguishes "ideas" from "phenomena" ("philosophy's founding opposition"), thus clears the way for a new kind of theological reflection that is not all "metaphysical" or winces from the indignities of "classical theism."

Deconstruction comes forth as a potent challenge to process theology, not because it has carved a new trajectory, but because it cuts many on the same leading grooves. In essence, deconstruction accomplishes at the critical level what process thinking has labored for within its own ambit of theological naturalism and metaphysical idealism. The crypto-orthodoxy that has developed within some cenacles of process theology, the flailing of an animus that was appropriate in an earlier generation of controversy, the pounding of drumskins that have gone slack, may be dissolved if those thinkers set about to educate themselves in the crucial problems of language. In the words of Whitehead himself, "what looks like stability is a relatively slow process of decay."[16] The same might be said for the "stability" of the idea of process as it has been formulated in this era.

[16] Alfred North Whitehead, *The Function of Reason* (Boston: Beacon Press, 1966), p. 82.

SECTION IV

SCRIPTURE

CHAPTER 11

FROM TEXTUALITY TO SCRIPTURE:
THE END OF THEOLOGY AS "WRITING"*

". . . when rightly understood, the infinite significance of the Holy
Scriptures is not in contradiction to its hermeneutical limitations."
—FRIEDRICH SCHLEIERMACHER

"Now to preach the kingdom of God is nothing else than to preach
the gospel, in which is taught the faith of Christ by which alone
God dwells and rules in us. But the doctrines of men do not
preach about faith, but about eating, clothing, times, places,
persons, and about purely external matters which are of no profit
to the soul."
—MARTIN LUTHER

Even though they convey succinctly what the Reformation of the sixteenth century was fought over, Luther's words are strange to us. Stranger
still is this carefully honed dialectic of "faith" and "doctrines of men." For the
post-Romantic grounding of all "faith statements" in historical and linguistic
webworks of meaning has thrown us back unconditionally on certain theological postures corresponding to such "doctrines."

We know that if representations of ultimate reality are "projections," as
Feuerbach first contended, and theological locutions amount to "analogies,"
in David Tracy's words, then Luther's language of faith cannot be said to have
any privileged semantic status, and the notorious "Protestant principle"
becomes a *caput mortuum*. The Protestant principle, however, retains its
relevance if only because it backlights the fundamental dilemma of the
theologian in the waning era of modernity—the transcendental in contradis-
tinction to the mere historical role of the "Word of God." Christian liberalism, especially during the past two decades, has sought to avoid the
transcendental question by contriving a dogma of cultural perspectivalism
that has its earliest origins in the method of Wilhelm Dilthey. In this
connection it has become fashionable to say that theology is no longer
constitutive or constructive, but "hermeneutical." Furthermore, a her-

*This chapter first appeared as an essay in *Semeia*.

meneutical theology of this order is allegedly fashioned from the inexhaustible mirror play of textual elements strands, literary remains, and socio-
linguistic ensembles—what the post-structuralists have felicitously termed
the "formation."

A hermeneutical theology of this order is essentially a normative version
of *Religionswissenschaft*, the "science of religion", as a methodology elaborated in German universities during the nineteenth century. Such a theology
draws together the aggregates of symbolic givens and determines their
integral nature, which then becomes the basis for making judgements about
the "divine display" through the windows of historical particularity. The
approach, again, was made routine during the Romantic period. We find its
quintessential experession in Herder. Finally, the sentiment is consummated
in Hegel's metaphysics of itinerant reason. At the foundational level such a
hermeneutics is conceived as far more than the art of reading texts. It
becomes an archaeology—and therefore an ongoing meditation—of the phenomenal world itself. It rests on Gadamer's "polarity of familiarity and
strangeness,"[1] serving as a probe that goes behind all representations.
Modern hermeneutics, as Ricoeur has shown, has its genesis in the nineteenth century quest for understanding not the letter, but the total *human*
world in which literacy is generated as one among many puzzling signs and
tokens. It is "necessary", Ricoeur notes, "to push the central *aporia* of
hermeneutics further by considering the decisive development . . . of a
greater *universality*, which prepares the way for the displacement of epistemology towards ontology."[2]

The hermeneutical character of contemporary theology, first codified in
the later Tillich, can be derived explicitly from the move away from all forms
of confessionalism, from theories of religious knowledge, toward the deeper
"gnosis" of ontological comprehension. A hermeneutical theology, which
germinated in nineteenth century historicism and the sundry efforts at
historical "understanding", could only have emerged out of what was an
anthropologically informed *philosophy of religion*. According to Tillich, "theology is the normative and systematic presentation of the concrete realization
of the concept of 'religion'."[3] And religion is the manifestation through
symbolic forms, including myths, of the unity of life itself, of the "holy". A
hermeneutical theology maintains the semblance of the traditional preoccupation with the transmundane while, in fact, it is bent upon exploring
indefinitely the realm of the empirical. Such a theology is but a somewhat
baroque taxonomy of religious emblems, a scholastic kind of illuminism. The

---

[1] Hans Georg Gadamer, *Truth and Method* (New York: Crossroads, 1982), p. 262.
[2] Paul Ricoeur, *Hermeneutics and the Human Sciences: Essays on Language, Action, and Interpretation* (Cambridge: Cambridge University Press, 1981), p. 48.
[3] Paul Tillich, *What is Religion?* (New York: Harper & Row, 1973), p. 33.

text is but a cipher for other texts. And behind the texts lurks perhaps the abyss of unchartered "meaning" itself.

It is in this setting that the so-called "problem" of the text arises. Classical theology has always been concerned with rendering its texts in a manner that was historically intelligible and epistemologically coherent. But it has only been in what has perhaps prematurely been dubbed the "post-Christian" epoch that the text as text can be made an issue. The problem of the text is both a logical concomitant and an evolutionary sequel to the loss of the significance of scripture. And with the loss of the sense of scripture vanishes Luther's dichotomy between faith and human doctrine. At the same time, however, it is only such a dichotomy that ultimately commissions us to resolve the problem of the text. As the curator of symbols and the regulator of texts, hermeneutics must have proceeded somehow from the position that *particular* texts have scriptural integrity. What do we mean by this distinction? We must first clarify what is meant by scripture versus text.

Oddly, but not absurdly, the problem of scripture has its beginnings in the various mystifications posed by the text. A text is a complete presentation, an embroidery of appearances, as in the Greek etymon *texere*. "Text" is also connected orthographically to the term *tekhne*—hence "technics" or "technology". A third kind of archaic cognate is the term *tegere*—to "cover" or "conceal." Thus "textuality" is intimately associated with phenomenality. But the phenomenality of the text is not the same as the phenomenality of nature. Just as *techne* and *physis* constitute, for Heidegger, entirely different epochs in the sphere of ontology, so textual interpretation and natural history each have a different "epistemology." The problem of the text, as Gadamer has indicated, actually comes from the Romantic preoccupation with historical contingency as well as the early nineteenth century endeavor to find a metaphysical standpoint for the investigation of culture. Hence, Ricoeur's multi-facted attempt to meld hermeneutics with the human sciences is but the grand outworking of the previously unconscious Romantic enterprise.

The text shows itself as text once historical self-reflection has peremeated the adventure of inscription and interpretation. Derrida's program of deconstruction betokens the final moment in the progressive self-portrayal of the text. It is hermeneutics that has lost its enthrallment with history, which is exactly what happened during the French structuralist interlude, and must fall back upon the solipsism of reading and writing. If classical hermeneutics purports to obtain a first-order system of representations for the second-order phenemonality of literature, then in Derrida the referential thrust is toward the temporal displacement of language itself, toward meaning that is alienated and not recovered. That is the precise significance of Derrida's view of deconstruction as "double science." Interpretation does not unmask the phenomenon. In a trenchant sense it leaves intact the "covering" (*teguement*) that is in the text. What it does is to deracinate language and

expose it as text so that its semantics now is no longer a function of metaphysics, but of what Derrida calls the "liminal space" that "is thus opened by
an inadequation between the form and the content of discourse or by an
incommensurability between the signifer and the signified."[4]

In short, any hermeneutical exercise today is confronted by the sheer
facticity of texts which, in turn, springs from the total default of innocence
that has occurred since the completion of the modern cycle of historico-
critical understanding. It is this understanding that has disclosed all texts as
techne, as artifice. The act of canonization, which in an earlier age constituted a response to the suggestion of the "artificial" (i.e., the apocryphal)
and therefore merely "textual" character of certain religious documents,
would be a feckless strategy. For canonization, like creedalism, presupposes
an ideality anterior to the phenomenality of the inscription, a superior
denotation for historically contingent writing. Canonization, which occurs in
all literary ventures, rests on a deference to the primordial authority of
discourse. But when history inundates the letter, the canon is washed out.

At the same time, the canon is not necessarily what make the text a
scripture. Luther surely did not desire to couple faith with scriptural authority because the latter had somehow been ordained as the axial reference
point in the legacy of Christendom. Quite the contrary! For Luther, the
proclamation of *sola fide* ("by faith alone") was endued with the passion for
personal intimacy with the God of tradition, whose face remained veiled by
the literality of the canon itself. If Erik Erikson is correct in his well-known
appraisal of Luther's thought in relation to his biography, then the latter's
tutoring in Occam's nominalism, combined with his mystical and introspec-
tive tendencies comparable to what could be found in the late Medieval
devotional schools, made it impossible for him to treat "Scripture" as a
realistic touchstone for theology.[5] Instead, Luther could only appropriate the
grammatological dimension in religious thought as something that abolished
itself in order to secure the very *presence* of what could not be merely
encoded in writing—the incarnate *logos,* the living Christ. If one reads
Luther's polemics carefully, one obtains the distinct impression that the issue
is not human versus divine prerogatives so much as it is the hermeneutical
primacy of original language as opposed to the paltry *mimesis* of theological
construction. This motive is clear in Luther's treatise of 1539 *On the Councils
and the Church* in which he ridicules Catholic efforts since Augustine to
"harmonize" the scriptures and states baldly that "a canonist is nothing but
an ass." Scripture, for Luther, has what nowadays we might call a "primal"
intent. According to Luther: "Thus Scripture, too, must remain master and

[4] Jacques Derrida, *Dissemination,* trans. Barbara Johnson (Chicago: University of Chicago
Press, 1981), p. 18.
[5] See Erik Erikson, *Young Man Luther: A Study in Psychoanalysis* (New York: W.W. Norton,
1962).

judge, for when we follow the brooks too far, they lead us too far away from the spring, and lose both their taste and nourishment, until they lose themselves in the salty sea, as happened under the papacy."[6] It would not be going too far to say that the Lutheran idea of Scripture has prevailed in German thought from Hamann's obsession with an *Ursprache,* or "primal language," through Freud's notion of overdetermination of speech, to Heidegger's urging us toward "originary" language. Faith in the Lutheran sense is both an archaeology and an ontology; and it is this archaeology which converts the text into scripture, parlaying in the end what Bultmann, the last great Lutheran exegete, termed the *Sprach-ereignis,* the "language event."

But it is our historicism as applied to textual problems that has rendered such an archaeology, let alone an ontology, suspect. Historicism has become our modern, post-dogmatic habit of canonizing the work of interpretation. And it is this canonization of scriptural wording in accordance with historical usage, together with its purely semiotic format, that has brought back the conciliar or pre-Reformation style of hermeneutics. Certainly if the conciliar style were not in the ascendancy, we would not have the current, high-purposed, but misguided attempts to rewrite the Bible according to gen-derless grammar. And the conciliar style can only be the culmination of a long era of historicist verdicts, which have effaced all vestiges of the text's originary significance in favor of its cultural import. "Scripture" can only be tampered with, and rephrased by, socially conscious church committees once it has been depotentiated as scripture, once it is perceived no longer as the *fons et origo* of faith, but as a temporally scarred palimpsest, as text qua text.

Historicism, however, is a spurious hermeneutic. Indeed, it cannot pass muster as a hermeneutic at all, inasmuch as it merely constitutes chains of discourse without accomplishing the "fusion of horizons" that Gadamer has shown is indispensible to all credible interpretation. Philology, for example, cannot yield the elusive aim we call "meaning" any more than vital statistics can give us an "event." Philology only discloses for us strands of historical syntax. For interpretation we require a *tertio comparationis.* And what we know as components of scripture demanding historical intervention are themselves constituted by different horizons, different "preconcepts" in Gadamer's terms, which can be stropped down into one set of linear asser-tions through historicist reductionism.

Still, within the Western theological tradition all valorization of the religious text using the norm of scripture has been essayed in terms of the metaphysics of presence. For that traditional scripture is the text understood as a manifestation of the trans-textual, of the *logos.* The very idea of scripture, which is not uniquely Christian, derives from the primitive realization that

---

[6] Martin Luther, *Selected Writings,* edited by Theodore Tappert (Philadelphia: Fortress Press, 1967), IV, 212.

all language surpasses itself. The self-surpassing character of language has
been the most important discovery of phenomenology; and it gives the lie to
conventionalist, or sociological, theories of meaning which hold that words
signify primarily by their function within a system of semantic transactions or
operations. According to linguistic phenomenology, scripturality is the nimbus surrounding the word in its immediate presentation. That is the fundamental insight behind Heidegger's delphic saying "language speaks."
Language speaks, explains Merleau-Ponty, because "statements claim to
unveil the thing itself; language goes beyond itself toward what it signifies."[7]
The reification of the semantic act in which the letter is surpassed by the
semantic objective, the reference by the referent, is the source of the
metaphysics of presence. The text, if it has not been routinized, appears as
God's word.

But the metaphysics of presence—or more specifically the theology of
"God's word"—may be more closely related to the psychology of the
numinous and the mystique of hieroglyphs than what actually compels faith.
Luther may have been searching for the origins of true doctrine, but scripture itself has its genesis in something we call "revelation," in the saying of
the unsaid. That is where the philosophy of Derrida currently assumes
cardinal importance.

Derrida alone and the "method" of deconstruction, contrary to its current modest pride of place in post-theological dabbling with theology,[8] can
never be conscripted for the sake of preserving the re-presentation of essential meaning in the text, what during the Bultmannian era was innocently
known as the "kerygma". What Derrida has made explicit is the recognition
that textual studies by themselves are self-referring. All metaphysical, or
"theological", projects must somehow be grafted onto them. Metaphysics
since Aristotle has been the science of the identical. Deconstruction, which
actually has its origins in Nietzsche's assaults on Platonic formalism by
supplanting argument with parabolic anomaly, is the disclosure of difference.
And the movement of difference, according to Derrida, occurs within the
skein of repetitions, substitutions, word plays, and exchanges that emerges
as the process of reading and writing, or convergently as "interpretation."

The text merely bends back upon itself in what Derrida refers to as "the
dissimulation of the woven texture" that can "take centuries to undo its web."
Thus it must be the true confession of all hermeneutical philosophy that "to a
considerable degree, we have already said all we meant to say."[9] The unsaid
is said in the very instant of displacement, whereby all literalism is overcome

---

[7] Maurice Merleau-Ponty, Signs, trans. Richard C. McCleary (Evanston, IL: Northwestern
University Press, 1964), p. 81.
    [8] See Mark C. Taylor, Deconstructing Theology, American Academy of Religion Studies in
Religion No. 28 (Chico, CA: Scholars Press, 1982).
    [9] Dissemination, p. 65.

by the fact that writing renders impossible the rescue of presence. And the impossibility of rescue indicates that the text as the seemingly indeterminate web of writing suffices as the domain of the "sacred." It is Derrida's obsession with the text as text, and not as the threshhold of the numinous, that has prompted various critics to identify his style as "Rabbinic." For Derrida, the text is established with the divorce of writing from speech, which harbors the illusion of presence. Thus, the destruction of that illusion, suggests Taylor, may engender "the possibility of . . . a writing that is not in the service of speech but 'is' nothing other than scripture."[10] How can scripture be constituted, if it be understood in Taylor's eyes, as a kind of unbounded textuality in which presence has wholly vanished, in which there can be discerned no longer the Lutheran *revelatum?*

It is here that we can draw a subtle, but extremely critical distinction between the Lutheran concept of faith as appropriation of the kerygmatic content and the Reformed attitude that "the finite cannot contain the infinite," such as occurs in the early Barth. Especially in Barth's *Epistle to the Romans* we find what I shall refer to as the "hermeneutic of the infinite," which substitutes for the kind of Lutheran/Bultmannian hermeneutic of the immediate, deriving from the metaphysics of presence.

The hermeneutic of the infinite is contained expressly in the notorious Barthian principle of "KRISIS", where time-tested structures and organons of human experience are divulged as blunt fabrications, where historical life itself—which was the protological "text" for Dilthey—is apprehended as having "meaning as a parable of a wholly other world."[11] It is configured in the Kierkegaardian critique of the "speculative distraction" that arises from the Hegelian fascination with the transformations of culture, a distraction that misses "the incommensurablity that subsists between an historical truth and an eternal decision."[12] It is the principle of incommensurability bodied in the *finitum non capax*, or in the Kierkegaardian disavowal of historicism, that sets the backdrop for the passage from the mere hermeneutical enterprise to a confrontation with the "wholly other." For it is the presentation as what Steven Smith has called an "argument to the other,"[13] a movement of discourse away from secure rules of inference to the entertainment of the paradoxical relation, that confirms the basis of the distinction between text and scripture.

Whether we are speaking of the classic document or the entire warp of representations, glyphs and ciphers comprising a "formation," the text as the

[10] Mark C. Taylor, "Altizer's Originality: A Review Essay", *Journal of the American Academy of Religion* 52 (1984): 583.

[11] Karl Barth, *The Epistle to the Romans*, trans. Edwyn C. Hoskyns (London: Oxford University Press, 1968), p. 107.

[12] Soren Kierkegaard, *Concluding Unscientific Postscript*, trans. David F. Swenson (Princeton, NJ: Princeton University Press, 1968), p. 90.

[13] See Steven Smith, *The Argument to the Other* (Chico, CA: Scholars Press, 1983).

proper object of interpretation, which achieves its transcendent dimension at
the moment Derrida calls "difference," is forever indited within a matrix of
signifiers. Scripture, on the other hand, is eternally open to an entirely
divergent "order" of possibilities—Kierkegaard's "infinite qualitative difference." Therefore, when Taylor suggests that the deconstruction of the
theological motive, which in turn abolishes the semantics of presence, must
lead to a new avowal of "scripture," he is really talking about what the French
term *écriture*—writing as Derrida's "supplementary double," as the order of
appearance, as mime—rather than about *scriptura*—writing as the formal
composite of language that "means" other than itself.

And so in a very important sense the distance between text and scripture
seems at first glance to turn on the hermeneutical choice between the post-
structural glorification of language as self-implicated process, as a game of
icons, and what is really a neo-Heidegerrian theory of discourse as *incarnation*. If we examine the classical meaning of *scriptura*, we find that it refers to
the densification of word and text into a public *de-scription*, the metamorphosis of mere writing into the document. Furthermore, the document
becomes the repository of presence that stands wholly apart from the act of
writing which gave it body. The document is charged with the sense of
"otherness". That is why "scripture" has always been gilded and illuminated
by monastic scribes. Scripture is the "book", and the book is not simply the
material ensemble of inscriptions. It is a true theophany. "Book" is etymologically connected to "beech", an "edible tree" (cf. the Greek root
phago-). Thus the book is the tree, the symbol of life, that is ingested as a
sacrament. Reading in the classical context is akin to the celebration of the
"mass", the assimilation of meanings, the consumption of the god, the
transfer of presence. It is clear that "deconstruction", which prophesies "the
end of the book," is founded upon the Hebraic passion for inconcolasm, for
de-situating holiness and making it a temporal disclosure. The semantics of
presence is really the ritual of the temple, trenching upon the very institu-
tion of idolatry.

But scripture also has another connotation that can be placed midway
between the classical model and the Derridean force of *ecriture*. Even as a
possible variant on the classical understanding, "scripture" can be construed
not as *ecriture* so much as *oeuvre*. The notion of the *oeuvre* has heavily
informed the less radical proponents of a post-structural hermeneutics,
particularly Ricoeur. For Ricoeur, all language, as opposed to writing by
itself, figures into the *oeuvre* or "work" of discourse. The "work" is what
gives language its foundation, its ontology. The Ricoeurian "work" is the
same as the Heidegerrian *poiesis* or "poetizing", a coming to presence
through language rather than the installation of presence in the book. The
work constitutes an "outworking" of the transtemporal within the rhythm of
language. As with the "scriptural" dimension of the Biblical word, it is a
manifestation of the *kairos*, the "fullness" within the flux of the historical.

The work means that the text, which enjoys its own cultural privilege and autonomy, now parlays into a set of paradoxical references, which is actually a better way of grasping Ricoeur's idea of the "surplus of meaning." And these paradoxical references—vectored on the one hand toward the synatx of common sensicality and on the other hand toward the indeterminacy of the unspoken—establish the language of the text as scripture.

For words become "scriptural", as we have argued, not because they are already canon, but because they reveal in their immedicacy what cannot be enclosed, or "inscribed", as part of discourse, Derrida's "mimesis" is an incomplete account of the self-surpassing properties of language, because it obscures the semantics of paradox as well as the hermeneutics of the infinite. Displacement is not equivalent, ontologically speaking, to transcendence. The current theological, or "a-theological" in Taylor's sense, fascination with deconstruction reflects an odd sort of neo-Wittgensteinian "bewitchment" with language itself, a kabbalistic enchantment with the letter.

But this enchantment can never be hermeneutics, nor theological work, nor the general resolution of the enigmas of language, for that matter. For such a resolution hinges on the realizing of the capacity of text to become work, "scripture" in its non-eidetic or past-canonical form. It was Ricoeur who first gave us the word "deconstruction," which designated the transit from Husserlian phenomenology to the critique of ideology, the dismantling of self-referential systems of subjective idealism and their replacement by the philosophy of language.[14] Moreover, it is the philosophy of language that, so far as the Ricoeurian effor to make language "mean more than it says" is concerned, leaves open the possibility of scripture. As Walter Lowe argues, the Reformed principle of *finitum non capax* ("finite not containing the infinite") is lodged at "the Ricoeurian center."[15] And that principle is what enables religious thinking to be emancipated from all forms of academic "superstition", including Hermeticism, psychologism, sociologism, positivism, subjectivism, and even the fashionable belletrism that has haunted us since the first annunciation of the "end of theology". If *hermeneutics per se* is engaged in the demystification of the text, then the hermeneutics of the infinite is what holds forth the option of regarding the text as scripture. For scripture is more than "writing", even though it is writing in both an historical and phenomenal sense that has constrained the discovery of the Kierkegaardian "paradox".

The paradox, the rupture of the "eternal", can only arise at the moment that the self-certainty of consciousness is "objectified," i.e., encounters itself

---

[14] See Paul Ricoeur, *The Conflict of Interpretations: Essays in Hermeneutics* (Evanston, IL: Northwestern University Press, 1974).

[15] See chapter 2 entitled "The Case of Paul Ricoeur" in Walter Lowe, *Evil and the Unconscious,* American Academy of Religion Studies in Religion No. 30 (Chico, CA: Scholars Press, 1983).

as heterology, in the writing, in the word as text. It was Kierkegaard's fundamental realization over against Hegel that the "return" of the subject to itself through the dialectical negation is possible only in the mirror of reflection, not in "existence." For it is writing that brings "spirit" into existence. That is why Kierkegaard was perhaps preoccupied with himself as an "author." Once the self-presence of the writer is annuled in the inscription, there can be no negation except through further writing. What Kierkegaard actually discerned is that Hegel's "speculative sentence" is impossible as sentence. The act of predication as an "othering" of the subjective contents belongs within the domain of logical inference, which in turn depends upon the sequential, not circular, movement of writing, i.e., the self-limiting continuum of grammar. Hence for Kierkegaard, the theological radical, even the alleged canonicity of religious texts cannot be taken seriously. "The first dialectical difficulty with the Bible," wrote Kierkegaard, "is that it is an historical document; so that as soon as we make it our standard for the determination of Christian truth, there begins an introductory approximation process, and the subject is involved in a parenthesis whose conclusion is everlastingly prospective."[16]

Derrida's "supplement" is Kierkegaard's "parenthesis." The parenthesis follows upon the vanishing of the self-presence of the author. The crucial difference between Kierkegaard and Derrida, who are both anti-Hegelian, is that for the latter the self-presence of the author, "alienated" eternally from the text he composes, is the touchstone of "existence." In the universe of "deconstruction," however, it is the text that manifests and the author who is disclosed as having no substance. Kierkegaard's parenthesis is set off by the paradox of the relationship between time and eternity. Derrida's "grammatology" yields the supplement that cannot be viewed in contrast, because the "subject" that has been replaced is now totally effaced and forgotten. Grammatology is the world of the text which stands by itself because the portals of the infinite have all been closed up. The Kierkegaardian paradox alone allows for the confirmation of a "scriptural" valency within both the religious and literary syntax. But we must ask ourselves: does the affirmation of text as scripture, which demands faith and not interpretation, put to rout the entire "theological" program of modernity, which has sought to "make sense" out of the most ancient and holy Word of God?

Speaking from a purely grammatical standpoint, there can be no such thing as "God's Word." Theological hermeneutics from Justin Martyr to Bultmann has been constituted as a privileged task, because of the tacit assumption that there was such a "content" to be rendered intelligible. But if we have learned anything from post-structural criticism, it is that a proper iconoclasm within the theory of language demands we discharge all claims of "content," "presence", or "subject" as phantoms of discourse. The text

---

[16] *Concluding Unscientific Postscript*, p. 38.

remains the given. Scripture is the hermeneutical discernment that the text as a finite system of inscription is somehow charged with the infinite. But that possibility can only be seriously countenanced if we understand that the study of religious and symbolical language, whether it be stated in the Wittgensteinian, Heidegerrian, or Derridean idiom, is not another disguised mode of metaphysics, but a propaedeutic to "faith" in the most profound and incommensuirable way. And it is the assertion of faith as the only genuine ground of a transcendental semantics that explains what we have meant all along by "the end of theology."

"Faith", which was Luther's watchword, of course has a greater force than any bare psychology that resists any enclosure of the infinite, whether it be through metaphysics, anthropology, or historicism. Ricoeur has given us what amounts to a theory of metaphorical disjunction that remains *inner-textual*. The theory offers a new philosophy of language free of Heideggerian obscurities as well as the kind of semiotic formalism so trendy in the last decade, which accounted for everything while explaining nothing. But a theory of metaphorical disjunction is not the same as a transcendental semantics. In contrast with T. M. van Leeuwen's provocative profile, the Ricoeurian model leaves us with an ontology, but not an *eschatology*.[17] For it is the nature of eschatology to oustrip all "grounds" of thinking, all starting points, even language itself. Ricoeur has not, in fact, been able to step out of Heidegger's shadow, where in *logos* and *ontos*, word and reality, inter-mingle, where mystery tortuously climbs toward utterance, where "lan-guage" is designed according to its primordial and pre-inscriptive architecture as the "house of Being." Ricoeur's semantics is Romantic lin-guistics that has been hybridized with the science of grammar. It is saturated with the symbology of archaic striving, the Romantic eros, the Nietzschean "will to power" which Heidegger recognized as the drive behind all meta-physics.

As Van Leeuwen says of Ricoeur, "philosophy understands faith pri-marily in terms of the desire to be."[18] But that is to confuse religion with faith. Barth's indictment of "religion" should be read carefully again by all theological thinkers and writers. Religion, as we have known since Auguste Comte, is actually something pre-metaphysical. At a semantic level it is the return of the represeed. It is the Dionysian force that impinges upon the Apollonian coherence of the text. Hence, if we are to move beyond theology to writing not merely as "text/techne", but as scripture, we must go beyond the Nietzchean struggle between intelligence and opacity, between form and chaos. Our intelligence must not be an apology for the occult, which is precisely why a new "philosophical theology," or even a serious Biblical

[17] See Theodor Marius van Leeuwen, *The Surplus of Meaning: Ontology and Eschatology in the Philosophy of Paul Ricoeur* (Amsterdam: Rodopi, 1981).
[18] Van Leeuwen, p. 187.

methodology, must absent itself from that curious and littered archaeological deposit we call "religious studies."

Perhaps such a theology in its fascination with the forms of language, experience, and of culture could recall Barth's long-neglected reminder that all "religious" reflection must shatter against the "No" of God. For the divine negation, which Barth has expressed dogmatically and metaphorically, is what we mean by the hermeneutics of the infinite. And it is the hermeneutics of the infinite that comes to reign only when theology is ending and theological thinking is dawning, when the parable has obliterated all Pharasaic and scribal (i.e., "academic") preconceptions, when the "Kingdom of God", and not the vanished author of the text, is present amid the grief of absence. The sentimentality of absence, as opposed to the celebration of the kingdom, is nonetheless dependent upon a peculiar vision of temporality. And it is this sentimentality, best described as the piety of the secular, which must be overcome if theological thinking is to rise from the rubble of befuddled triviality.

The textuality of the divine, which implies the re-appropriation of scripture in a genuine, *de-constructed* sense, appears before us if, and only if, the relationship between time and eternity is understood anew, pre-eminently as a thinking of what thought has heretofore not thought through. Theological thinking, in effect, begins with the eschatology of that thought which has been determined as the foundations of all "fundamental theology". Theological thinking, as Hegel knew, must plunge into time as the depth of its "unthought-most" possibilities, where scripture as the disclosure of the infinite is read from the very grammar of a still obscure, and perhaps "archaic", history.

CHAPTER 12

TIME AS THE UNTHOUGHT THOUGHT OF THOUGHTS:
AN ESCHATOLOGICAL OVERTURE

"*. . . History,* is a *conscious,* self-*mediating* process—Spirit emptied out into Time . . . The realm of Spirits which is formed in this way in the outer world constitutes a succession in Time in which one Spirit relieved another of its charge and each took over the empire of the world from its predecessor. Their goal is the revelation of the depth of Spirit . . ."

—G.W.F. Hegel

The enigma of time has bestirred both theologians and philosophers since the cockcrow of speculative idealism. Although the phenomenon of time itself has resisted the kind of finely stropped analysis with which philosophers have habitually engaged themselves, the question concerning temporal experience and temporal reality has overshadowed the Western intellectual tradition for millenia. Classical metaphysics was concerned with the problem of time as part of the larger riddle of the origin and purpose of motion itself. From Parmenides forward the question, *What is time?*, was usually positioned within the context of the problem of change, or more specifically mutation. The Greek presupposition was that the "existent" is identical with the ideal. Aristotle's oft-quoted comment that nature equals *morphe,* or "form", harbored an assumption that those things to be observed and studied by the "natural philosopher" were the enduring principles according to which the flux of becoming could somehow be regularized. Temporality, therefore, proved to be a tacit, if not compelling, metaphysical conundrum for the Greeks, because it showed itself as the very horizon within which all things fixed and permanent could be explained as undergoing perceptible alterations.

Plato, of course, did not come up with a satisfactory "solution" to dilemma comparable to Aristotle. Plato's resort in the *Timaeus* to the well-known "mythic" interpretation of time as a "moving" icon of the eternal reflected a profound sense of puzzlement on his part more than a deliberate metaphysical strategy. Plato's unwillingness to embrace the paradoxical character of the concept of time, chiefly because of his adherence to the

Parmenidean ontology, may have weakened his overall contribution to subsequent philosophical progress. Aristotle, on the other hand, recognized that
temporality is not simply some sort of strange sigil for the unchangeable. The
"real" is inseparable from the fact of movement. Its supreme representation
is a revolving sphere. By superadding the property of rotary motion to the
Eleatic notion of "Being" as a perfect sphere, Aristotle helped wean early
metaphysical speculation away from the beguiling view of truth as "permanent presence," if we may employ Heidegger's phrasing.

Ancient philosophy struggled long with the ontological status of *ta
gignomena*, "that which is becoming." But if we disperse the mists of all-too-
familiar metaphysical folderol and inquire about what precisely gave rise to
the lofty debates launched by the pre-Socratics, we must nurse the suspicion
that Greek thinking was actually laboring to construct a logic of temporality.
The ascendancy of the noun substantive form in both Greek and Latin syntax
may, if one hypothesis of modern linguistics is accurate, have contributed
largely to the identification of "what is" with that which is prior to all
predications or modifications. Greek philosophy was essentially a deductive
system, unrolling the meanings and implications of terms from general
definitions and presuppositions. Such a predilection is conveyed in Aristotle's dictum that "all teaching and intellectual learning come about from
already existing knowledge."[1] The belief that contingent knowledge can
always be derived by either dialectic or demonstration from what Aristotle
termed "reputable opinions" was indelibly chiseled in Greek philosophy.
Thus the supreme subject of Greek reflection turned out to be that locution
which signified the enduring itself, "Being qua Being," or that which stands
alone without any qualification or limitation.

Greek metaphysical discourse sufficed to describe the eternal over
against the temporal, primarily because of the difficulty of expressing the
manifest phenomenon of change through the dominant grammar of substance. The "discovery" of time as succession in the classical world has
usually been explained by cultural anthropologists and historians alike as
some mysterious theological breakthrough. Yet it may be that the typifica-
tions of time, now as well as then, may have more to do with the philosophy
of language than with the philosophy of nature. Indeed, they may be more to
do with basic patterns of reference and signification common to a culture
than with some postulated mythic *a priori* whereby time is grasped as
eternal recurrence, or as divine action resulting either in the maintenance of
cosmic order or in catastrophe.[2]

---

[1] Aristotle, *Posterior Analytics* 71a1.

[2] One of the most influential works to offer a structural reading of the archaic time sense is, of
course, Mircea Eliade's *The Myth of the Eternal Return*, trans. Willard R. Trask (Princeton, NJ:
Princeton University Press, 1954). Eliade, however, is quite straightforward in his admission
that he is writing a "philosophy of history" and that he is defending "archaic ontology" against

Time in the ancient setting was apprehended as a kind of plenitude which burst through, like water that has built up pressure behind a levee, into discrete moments. This mythic conception of temporal reality was often intertwined with the cycles of natural fertility, or to the destinies of nations. But at the same time it centered upon the vague symbolization of time as substance, as the unmoved which produces movement. Such a mythic vision is strongly implied in Aristotle's well-known meditation in the *Physics*, where he characterizes time as "a measure of motion and of being moved," and as "the motion which will measure the whole motion, as the cubit does the length by determining an amount which will measure out the whole."[3] A more discreet reading of the lengthy passage in which Aristotle holds forth what this definition indicates that time in the *Physics* amounts to what we would today call the "transcendental condition" or perceptual horizon of change as a whole. The phenomenonality of change, for Aristotle, is marked out by the sequence of immediate moments, by a stream of "nows". Time as we experience it is akin to phalanxes of soldier marching past our angle of sight, which is fixed on one particular spot in the parade route. However, Aristotle notes, our fundamental idea of time entails the span of past and future that stretches far beyond the present. How do we account for time in this respect? Perceived as opposed to conceived time, or better yet the "physical" and "metaphysical" modes of the temporal, are only distinguishable from a logical standpoint, according to Aristotle. Time penetrates our thought and our experience. Time is an instance of what in Aristotelian metaphysics is called "primary being", inasmuch as it contains all existing things undergoing transformation, which move from potentiality to actuality.

The signal achievement of classical metaphysics was to have extrapolated from the "esthetic" awareness of time as bare succession to a higher-grade, or what we would nowadays regard as "scientific", appreciation of temporal reality. Newton's rather tendentious construct of "absolute time", of which passing moments or temporal representations are but fragments, did not constitute any noticeable advance beyond the thought of Aristotle. Even Einstein's portrayal of time as the fourth "dimension" of an integral, space-time manifold can be construed as a kind of mathematicization of the Aristotelian idea of a superordinate form, or "measure", of motion.

What might best be described as the "deconstruction" of the metaphysical category of time commences with Kant, although it is also fair to say that the eschatological theme of the "end of days" that predominated in Judeao-Christian literature provided the critical level of consciousness which

---

the "historicizing" character of both modern and Christian thought. In the foreword Eliade writes that "the cardinal problems of metaphysics could be renewed through a knowledge of archaic ontology." (p. x) Perhaps much of our contemporary speculation on the patterning of time in bygone cultures conceals this kind of antiquarianism.

[3] Aristotle, *Physics* 220b33–221a2.

eventually undermined the Greek philosophy of substance. Deconstruction and the *temporalization of time*, as becomes explicit in the existential phenomenology of Heidegger, are intimately bound up with each other. Heidegger's explication of the metaphysical concept of time in tandem with his analysis of human finitude, which he carried out in his groundbreaking work *Being and Time*, must be glimpsed against the backdrop of the modern philosophical endeavor to "overcome" metaphysics, predating existentialism itself.[4] Kant's revolutionary declaration that "time is not something existing by itself, or inherent in things as an objective determination of them" not only exploded the presumptions of classical philosophy, which had reached a summit in Newton, it also shifted the grounds concerning how one reflected upon temporal experience from metaphysics to psychology.[5] For Kant, "time is nothing but the form of internal sense, that is, our intuition of ourselves, and of our internal state." Therefore, it "cannot be a determination peculiar to external phenomena."[6]

The notice that time calculations and anticipations principally involve the "internal sense" coincided with the discovery toward the end of the eighteenth century of temporal relativity and the vastness of the temporal spectrum. One of the pivotal factors in this shift of thinking was the relaxing of the seemingly invincible grip that geometry held over scientific cosmology. What Pascal dubbed *l'esprit geometrique* had reigned supreme for a century and a half in science, in philosophy, and (if we consider religious dogmatism as an instance of pure formalism) in theology. As historian of science G. J. Whitrow observes, the idea of time as geometrical locus and a substantivist metaphysics frequently go hand in hand.

By the late Enlightenment, however, and in the aftermath of the spread of Newtonian mechanics, the geometrical vision of science gave place to the algebraic model, which was founded on the descriptions of motion. The great physicist William Hamilton surmised that algebra itself must be a "pure mathematical science of time"[7], which shows that the structure of temporality is somehow mirrored in arithmetic operations. In fact, the Greek words for "number" (*arithmos*) and the "flow of time" (*rhythmos*) are etymologically quite similar. Aristotle himself, before reaching his "metaphysical" conclusions about the universal nature of time, opined that time could essentially be reduced to counting or numerality.[8] Since counting, as Aristotle himself observed, depends on a subjective attendance to the pag-

[4]Although the word "overcoming" metaphysics was first coined by Heidegger, the notion corresponds the project of most twentieth century philosophy in both the empiricist and Continental traditions.

[5]Immanuel Kant, *Critique of Pure Reason*, trans. Max Mueller (Garden City, NY: Doubleday, 1966), p. 30.

[6]*Critique of Pure Reason*, p. 31.

[7]See G. J. Whitrow, *The Natural Philosophy of Time* (New York: 1961), p. 116.

[8]See Aristotle *Physics* 220b7–221a29.

eant of "nows", the phenomenality of time must be connected with what he called the "standpoint of the intellect". But the conviction that time belongs to the mind, and not to the world of objects, did not emerge until the Kantian period.

By the beginning of the Romantic era the philosophical problem of time had been recast as the question of the origins and evolution of the world. The fascination with time now appeared as an effort to probe into the obscurity of natural history, spurred in large part by the advances of archaeology and anthropology. European colonialism's encounter with remote and primitive peoples, together with the amassing of fossils, effectively dissolved all metaphysical boundaries governing the concept of cosmic time, which had been forged from Biblical stories and Greek speculation, and urged a new "mythic" estimation of temporal reality that allowed for possibilities and prospects heretofore unimaginable.[9] Indeed, the newly fashionable "idea of progress", which was in itself a grand myth replacing the Christian scheme of salvation, could only have emerged with the broad-reaching deconstitution of metaphysical thinking about time scales that got underway in the seventeenth century. The hermeneutical scaffolding for "overcoming" the metaphysics of time is, of course, established in Kant. In a posthumously published essay Kant explained what may be taken perhaps as the a central motivating element in the modernist assault on metaphysics. "Metaphysics completely distinguishes itself from all other sciences," Kant wrote, "in that it is the only one that can be presented in its entirety so that nothing remains for posterity to add so as to extend its content."[10]

The Kantian critique of metaphysics as a closed society of mutually interlocking ideas which cannot be amended or improved, thereby precluding any possibility of "progress" through history, cleared the way for a wholly unprecedented "interpretation" of time that looked backward into a fathomless past and forward into an apparently illimitable future. The heuristics of Aristotelian inference, which created the kind of *a priori* reasoning in metaphysics challenged by Kant, were closely related to the axiomatic structure of Euclidean geometry. All justifiable or "scientific" knowledge, therefore, is both hierarchical and self-authenticating. Questionable propositions can either be verified or falsified through analysis of the manner in which they can be derived from the most basic kinds of logical statements.[11]

---

[9] For a detailed and highly useful reference in intellectual history concerning how the modern time sense developed, see Paolo Rossi, *The Dark Abyss of Time: The History of the Earth & The History of Nations from Hooke to Vico*, trans. Lydia G. Cochrane (Chicago: University of Chicago Press, 1984). A more limited, but highly insightful study is Merle L. Perkins, *Diderot and the Time-Space Continuum: His Philosophy, Aesthetics and Politics* (Oxford: The Voltaire Foundation, 1982).

[10] Immanuel Kant, *What Real Progress Has Metaphysics Made in Germany Since the Time of Leibniz and Wolff?*, trans. Ted Humphrey (New York: Basic Books, 1983), p. 173.

[11] For a discussion of the connection between Aristotelian logic and geometry, see Lawrence

Because Euclidean geometry arose as a topological form of symbol management, it could in no way account for the data of time and motion, which
would have to await the invention of the calculus two millenia later. Aristotle's
solution to the problem of time, which he identified as a type of "metric",
remained sufficient, so long as the psychological and historical conditions of
explanation were overlooked by philosophy. But the eighteenth century
gestation of what would eventually be dubbed the "human sciences", which
investigated the evolution of cultural artifacts, linguistic habits, and social
representations, mandated that any science of time would inquire assidu-
ously into the sources of temporal experience itself.

Kant's assertion that "in time alone is reality of phenomena possible"[12]
marked a telling departure from the metaphysics of eternal substance, which
had been the touchstone of both philosophical and theological thinking in the
past. For Kant, temporality and phenomenality are one in the same. To say
that something is real and intelligible means that it must be apprehended
within the milieu of "internal sense." Furthermore, a temporal phenomenology becomes the new "critical" standpoint from which any kind of
pronouncements or judgements concerning "objective" reality may be offered. The position of theological thinking itself, hitherto subordinate to a
substantive metaphysics, is registered in terms of the self-reflection of consciousness. It comes as no surprise that the subsequent Hegelian endeavor
to do "metaphysics" as an unfurling of the figurations of consciousness rests
squarely upon the insight that time is the sufficient reason for the presencing
of the world itself. God can no longer be viewed as a supreme entity who
exists solely as the logical grounding of every mundane and supermundane
semantics. God is the "representation" of *Godness*, which in turn belongs to
the "transcendental" region of cognition. In the same fashion that time, as
Kant would argue, makes it possible for all appearances to appear, so the
divine is what we really are talking about when we refer to the temporalizing
of time. Emancipated from its metaphysical bondage, theological thinking
now thinks about temporality as what Heidegger would term the "worlding
of the world."

But this "worlding" is not cheap happenstance. Nor is it a password for
some kind of pseudo-logic and pseudo-science, of which the Heideggerian
agenda is routinely accused. The focus of theological thinking on temporal
reality denotes a movement beyond an obsolete theory of representation, or
picture of "Deity", and in the direction of a pure *hermeneutics of the holy*.
Following the epistemology of Husserl, who represents the historical bridge
between Kant and Heidegger, we say that every "object" to be intuited or
understood is pre-eminently a "temporal thing", a *res temporalis*. The

---

Sklar, *Space, Time, and Spacetime* (Berkeley, CA: University of California Press, 1974), p. 79ff.
See also Robert S. Brumbaugh, *Unreality and Time* (Albany, NY: State University of New York
Press, 1984), p. 107.
  [12]*Critique of Pure Reason*, p. 29.

"essence" or true meaning of everything which appears "in time" is *time itself*.[13]

Husserl, of course, was too distracted by his own neo-idealist interest in the formalism of all knowledge to embellish the importance of such a posture. But the consequence of such a claim cannot be overestimated. Whereas Kant had merely acknowledged the subjective character of time as the unifying principle of lived experience, Husserl showed how the structure of "time consciousness" turns out to be the cornerstone of a fundamental ontology. The argument has been picked up by Heidegger and given renewed emphasis. "The universal ontological function that Kant assigned to time at the beginning of his laying of the foundation of metaphysics," says Heidegger, "can be justified only if time itself in its ontological function, i.e., as the essential element of pure ontological knowledge, forces us to determine the essence of subjectivity more primordially than heretofore."[14] In other words, the "subjective" format of temporal experience is not an epistemological starting point at all, but amounts to a redefinition of the context in which an ontological understanding can be secured. Time is not a subjective condition of knowledge so much as it is the pre-conceptual, and henceforth post-metaphysical, horizon for all phenomena to manifest themselves.

Aristotle seems to have dimly conceived this state of affairs, but lacked the philosophical vocabulary to have made sense out of it. Thus the temporality of all things temporal, which are experienced only because they are "temporalized,", constitutes the genuine "transcendental" subject matter for a "first philosophy." But this first philosophy, or what might better be characterized as *primal thinking*, cannot be metaphysics in its conventional guise. While metaphysical argument is bound up with the logic of predication, primal thinking accosts us at the margins of discourse. Primal thinking is what we have called theological thinking; and theological thinking, if we are to make such a twist in our own reckoning, must in the concluding analysis contend with the essential meaning of temporality.

The same sort of discernment can be gleaned from the meditations of Augustine. Human existence, circumscribed within time, has as its aim the varieties of "temporal happiness," according to Augustine. The striving for temporal happiness, which holds out the possibility of the meaning of time itself, grows out of human desire. And desire can be targeted toward either worldly and ephemeral modes of satisfaction or toward the eternal Creator. When temporal desire finds satisfaction in the eternal, the very ambiguities of time are superseded. Thus, Augustine in his prayerful petition to God proclaims: "In the eternal Sabbath you will rest in us, just as now you work in

---

13 "The Thing in its ideal essence presents itself as *res temporalis*, in the *necessary "form"* of *Time*. . . We grasp in *"pure intuition"* . . . the "Idea" of temporality and of all the essential phases included in it." Edmund Husserl, *Ideas: General Introduction to Phenomenology*, trans. W. R. Boyce Gibson (New York: Collier Books, 1962), p. 383.

14 Martin Heidegger, *Kant and the Problem of Metaphysics*, trans. James S. Churchill (Bloomington, IN: Indiana University Press, 1962), p. 54.

us. The rest that we shall enjoy will be yours, just as the work that we now do
is your work done through us. But you, O Lord, are eternally at work and
eternally at rest. It is not in time that you see or in time that you move or in
time that you rest: yet you make what we see in time; you make time itself
and the repose which comes when time ceases."[15] The word "God" signifies
the eternity which has no significance apart from time. That eternity is not
some Platonic cloudland segregated from the kingdom of change by means of
the duplex logic of substance and shadow, universal and particular, being and
becoming. It is the indwelling "essence" of time in its coursing; it is the
temporality of what is temporal.

Yet the temporality of the temporal, to which theological thinking *intra
fide*, or "in faith", cleaves as the thought of thoughts remaining in certain
measure unthought, cannot be approached strictly by the way of "deconstructive" rhetoric. Deconstruction is to theological language as the
classical form of *via negativa* has been to theological speculation. It serves as
a safeguard against the prideful and reifying impulses of modern, humanist
ideology. If contemporary theology had not in the recent past run up against
its own "moment" of deconstruction, it would have been overrun with
legions of new "constructive" manias, brandishing everything from Marxist
economics to positivist semiotics. Deconstruction in theology has preserved
theological thinking from immolating itself on the pyre of a secular social
metaphysics with subtle, totalitarian shadows at the periphery. Nevertheless, deconstruction itself, which springs from the Heideggerian project of
finitizing the pseudo-eternal tokens of philosophic discourse, cannot play
proxy, as we have already indicated, for the task of thinking. Deconstruction
is to thinking as the miner's chisel is to gold-digging. The "end" of thinking is
that which must be somehow inscribed within the multiple contents of
thought. And if time is the content of theological thinking, inasmuch as it is
in its most primitive phenomenological meaning that within which all
thoughts are contained, then it must be thought through in a manner
appropriate to the traditions and symbols by which it has been vested.

The Western anchorage for theological thinking, as Dennis Baly has
noted, is the "God" Yahweh, whose legacy of self-disclosure is recollected in
the Old Testament scriptures. But the name Yahweh proves to be paradoxical, insofar as it is not a representation, or "name", at all. Whereas the
names of the gods who competed for attention with the Hebrew "God" can
be assimilated to certain instances of everyday language and experience, the
"name" Yahweh functioned in naming what was ultimately beyond names.
The viewpoint for the worship of Yahweh was not that of familiarity, but of
otherness.[16] The radical otherness of the divine in the religion of ancient

[15] Saint Augustine, *Confessions*, trans. R. S. Pine-Coffine (New York: Penguin, 1961), p. 346.
[16] See Dennis Baly, *God and History in the Old Testament* (New York: Harper & Row, 1976),
p. 11.

Israel, of course, has been the topic of theological discussion and commentary throughout the twentieth century. During the interlude of neo-Orthodoxy the notion of divine alterity became something of an obsession, and the word "otherness" a kind of rallying torch. But the category of otherness also has decided implications for theological thinking regarded, in keeping with our earlier suggestion, as a means of pondering the meaning and marrow of temporality. The otherness of Yahweh coincided with his transcendence of all localities and all spatial determinants. His "lordship" of historical events corresponded to a proprietary religious outlook, codified in the so-called "Deuteronomic history", which maintained that clashes of armies and intrigues of kings were somehow ciphers for the scarcely understood intentionality of the Almighty. Whereas the heathen gods ascended and fell with the empires for which they served as talismans, Yahweh's "will" was revealed as the very superstructure of historical change itself. Whereas the heathen gods, denigrated by the prophets as flimsy "idols," had their specific cults and territorial influence, Yahweh had a *story*. Moreover, that story was tantamount to what in both Greek and Latin was known as *historia*, which can be translated as "narrative" or the knowledge that comes through retelling. Human events by themselves are a farrago of fumes and clatter. The representation of the "deep structure" of distinct trains of events belongs to religion, which communicates them as legends and myths, as heroes and minor divinities, all of which embody in sensible garb what is abstruse and supersensible. The representation of the inner purpose of time itself is, in a profound manner of speaking, *beyond religion*. It is the intimation of otherness within the tightly stitched web of the phenomenal. It is, we might say, the story of stories.

If we are to comprehend from a philosophical, and by extension from a theological, angle what time is all about, we must pay heed, says Ricoeur, to the semantics of narrative. Every sort of "speculation on time," Ricoeur argues, "is an inconclusive rumination to which narrative activity alone can respond."[17] Ricoeur qualifies such a remark as follows: "to put it another way, *time becomes human to the extent that it is articulated through a narrative mode, and narrative action attains its full meaning when it becomes a condition of temporal existence.*"[18] The *hominization* of time, betokening what can be read in Heidegger as the *finitizing* of the metaphysical understanding of Being itself through its reduction to the vantage point of human temporality, has been Ricoeur's persistent concern. And it comports with Ricoeur's own stringent, and to a certain extent arcane, phenomenological program. Nonetheless, an observation must be made about Ricoeur's treatment of the philosophical issue of time, which outstrips his

---

[17] Paul Ricoeur, *Time and Narrative*, vol. 1, trans. Kathleen McLauhglin and David Pellauer (Chicago: University of Chicago Press, 1984), p. 6.

[18] *Time and Narrative*, p. 52.

own immediate agenda. The endeavor to make time intelligible in light of the structure of poetics, for which Ricoeur leans heavily on Aristotle, intimates that the *theological* inquiry into temporality must be closely affiliated with an archaeology of narrative discourse. For such discourse—whether we are confronting the pericopes of the Gospels, the strophes of Greek drama, or the fabulous embroiderings of a Hindu epic—reveals a mode of temporalization prior to the contrapuntal logic of metaphysical thought. The temporalization of narrative discourse, which at a semiotic level comprises a shattering of the chain of conventional signifiers and the efflorescence of more "rhythmic" patterns of meaning, is contingent upon a *philosophical* assent to the possibility of less bounded, i.e., not strictly predicative, forms of understanding. Such a possibility is sketched eloquently by Ricoeur, who makes a case for narrative understanding as an occasion of teleological understanding. Ricoeur's claim swivels on the observation that "there is no history of the present."[19] Teleological understanding requires an assessment of the tendencies and trajectories of the past along with their projection toward the future.

However, such an assessment is usually what come to be involved in historical interpretation and recounting. For there to be what we blithely term a "sense of history," there must be an ontological comprehension of the "terrain" of temporality so far as it extends "backwards" and "forwards" in time. Such a temporal field must be amenable to its own style of topological description, which is the role performed by narrative. The historical narrative, which constitutes a poetics of memory, serves to map what "has been" by employing the symbols of our imagined identity as well as our anticipations. The Gospel writers could not have told the "story" of Jesus without an expectation of its fulfillment in his historical return. Even today we cannot write the history of the American nation bereft of a script for its destiny. The distinction between standard and revisionist histories within the framework of American historiography often turns on a conflict of intramundane eschatologies. Predicate logic, on which the preponderance of Western metaphysical and philosophical disputation rests, is only capable of expliciting the "now", as Aristotle learned. We can make a judgement about something in the past, or in the future for that matter, but our semantic wherewithal is obtained through our knowledge of relations that exist at the moment. We cannot really "judge" the past except in the measure that we prescind entirely from the present, and at the juncture we are employing language that does not avoid, but in the most literal sense "surveys" time. *We are in the world of narrative.*

A co-ordination of the concept of time as the "transcendental" groundwork of perception with the historical consideration of time as the evolution of concealed purpose was attempted by Kant in his *Critique of Judgement.*

---

[19]*Time and Narrative*, p. 147.

Although Kant's accomplishment in this area can be found wanting from a purely philosophical point of view, we must salute him for his effort to show how the epistemology of everyday experience and the larger, "speculative" interpretation of both nature and history can be unified in a single, "critical" standard of exposition. The middle term between Kant's rudimentary theory of knowledge and his defense of teleology was the principle of the "imagination." The imagination, according to Kant, does not perform a "synthesis" of all perceptual givens, so that they will mesh with the inherent structure of human cognition, it also expands the intelligence to vast, speculative frontiers in promoting what was previously the "interest" of metaphysical reason under the aegis of reflection about historical time itself. Kant's doctrine of the "transcendental imagination" subsequently became a hermeneutical fulcrum for the Romantic idealists of the nineteenth century. And it would be proper to point out that much of twentieth century theology, following its own retreat from reason into the spurious haven of *religious thought* with its fairyland of "as if" beliefs and fictive truths, has found its own way again along what was, for Kant, essentially a detour. Even Ricoeur's investigation of narrative can be seen as a neo-Romantic quest for a metaphysics of the patently literary, an ontology of the figurative which does not need to entertain the troubling question of how temporalizing discourse, such as pertains to the language of narrative, actually discloses the temporal, or what is meant by temporality in its most rudimentary sense. Because twentieth century theology in its apologetic frenzy to light upon a workable "method of correlation" has virtually abdicated the task of thinking through to the depths of the linguistic structures, including dramatic narrative, it finds congenial, it has not been able to think the subject of time as a quintessential matter of theological thinking. It has not grasped that while time can indeed be temporalized by narrative discourse, what have called the temporality of the temporal—time as the *sine qua non* of time—as implied in the naming of the unnameable presence beyond and within time does not semantically conform to the structure of narrative. The structures of narrative must be "destructured" if we are to overcome even the metaphysics of Romantic imagination. Theological thinking must devote its attention to what Derrida refers to as the "ellipsis".

An ellipsis is a deliberate omission of a section of a sentence, or of a text. Derrida employs the metaphor of the ellipsis to communicate what happens with writing, particularly the writing of the text that crouches behind the formation of that to which we refer as our "theological tradition." Derrida characterizes writing as "a nonsymmetrical division designated on the one hand the closure of the book, and on the other the opening of the text."[20] This sort of statement has often been seized up by Derrida's own proselytes

---

[20] Jacques Derrida, *Writing and Difference*, trans. Alan Bass (Chicago: The University of Chicago Press, 1978), p. 294.

as a summons to halt the classical emulation of the great "work," the finished
volume or dissertation, and to discover what literary critic Roland Barthes
has termed "the pleasure of the text," a saturnalia of identifying and con-
struing signs as they appear everywhere. But Derrida is not seeking to
pronounce the end of writing and reading books so much as he is intent on
deconstructing the concept of the book itself. The "book", for Derrida,
indicates the putative permanence of presence made possible through the
power of literary inscription. The book signifies the "Word" that issued forth
"in the beginning," when it was first written down. Yet, says Derrida, the
moment we "return" to the book to read and interpret, as the written text
allows us to do, we are no longer immured within the book. In interpreting
we are "rewriting" the book, so to speak, and throughout this "movement of
succession" we find, according to Derrida who here adopts the language of
the poet Edmond Jabes, "God succeeds God, and the Book succeeds the
Book."[21] Furthermore, this "return" is "of an elliptical essence. Something
invisible is missing in the grammar of this repetition."[22] Interpretation,
which compasses both rereading and rewriting, recognizes that the "center"
of the text is missing. While the aim of interpretation is to ferret out the
kerygma of the text, the search winds up at the edge of an abyss. "God
succeeds God" in the sense that the hermeneutical quest for God, the
transcendental signified, concludes not with the realization of an order of
reference for the sign of signs, but an infinite omission. The text in all its
voluble neighborliness turns out to be an *eccentric* stranger. Still, the confrontation of theological thinking with this chasm, this aboriginal displacement, which inaugurates the phenomenon of textuality does not, and should
not, eventuate in silence. It is too easy to hold up Derrida as some philosophical executioner who cleverly tortures the word into oblivion. Derrida is the
late Rabbinic exegete, who substitutes for the long-forgotten and historically
opaque entrance of the wholly transcendent into time the sacrality of commentary, which plies interpretation upon interpretation, text upon text. The
object of commentary is neither "revelation" nor a form of what Derrida
refers to as "arche-writing," the origination of language itself. The object is
disclosed to be the vanishing of the object, an absence where presence was
assumed, the "ellipsis" of the text which through interpretation has been
contextualized.

Insofar as theological thinking recognizes the ellipsis in all foundational
materials, or conglomerates of discourse, from which it purports to remark
and expound, it has succeeded in "overcoming" the metaphysical obstruc-
tions that have existed since the first apologists. Like the Gospel parable
which in its dialectical intensity subverts the common order of religious
valuations buttressed by the authority of the "law," theological thinking in its

[21]*Writing and Difference*, p. 294.
[22]*Writing and Difference*, p. 296.

commitment to the deconstruction of the regime of signifiers receives the inbreaking of the "kingdom" of the unsaid. It is the totalitarianism of our twentieth century philosophy of language that has precipitated the present crisis of interpretation and stupefied the theological mind, so far as the "hearing" of anything beyond its own tired voice is concerned. According to Derrida, the passion for apodictic intelligibility, for eidetic clarity, for a total system of representation invents an "ultrastructuralism" where the geometry of the text is everything and its origin and teleology is suppressed.[23] The temporality of the text, which is at the same time its concealed potential for interpretation, can only be disclosed where language is listened to and relived, not as an endless repetition of the same, but as a speaking of the unspoken, or a thinking of the unthought, within the original fracture that Derrida calls the "ellipsis". Deconstruction of the text means that the freedom of the text, and therefore the freedom of the "One" who by evoking the text leaves only traces and not obvious signs within the text, can be sustained. It means also that "faith" can be preserved, if by such a word we have in mind the encounter of the human subject in its finitude with the otherness that is both absence and "total presence."

Faith belongs to history in the sense that it betokens a repudiation by theological thinking of the idols of socio-linguistic construction—whether they be the latest popular "world views", styles of social activism, or philosophical and literary methodologies—and an edging toward the ellipsis, where at once the darkness beyond the closure of the system of reference is made manifest, and the glory that suffuses the entire universe of historical and cultural possibilities can be glimpsed. The Derridaean moment of difference or, if we take one more step forward, the theological *thought of difference*, has epochal consequence for the historical epoch that has pronounced the death of God and the end of theology. For to think the difference, as Derrida invites us to do, between speech and phenomena, between representation and writing, between the thought of thoughts and the thinking of the unthought, is indeed to think into the abyss of time in the direction of the unthinkable origins of the temporal. All theology, therefore, is equivalent to a manner of thinking that we may designate *interpretatio temporalis*.

But such a move, as our initial quotation from the climax of Hegel's *Phenomenology* suggests, is not merely a stab at enlarging the province of quaint pursuits. It is truly a "revelation" of the "depths of Spirit", which drives us out of the temple of certainty into the wilderness of difference, where amidst a seemingly boundless hush the thinking of the divine may transpire. If the temporalization of the temporal belongs not to metaphysics but to narrative, and the turn of thinking to narrative discourse as a perpetual "retelling" of what has been told, means that the language of simple presence

---

[23] See *Writing and Difference*, p. 15ff.

must give place to an acknowledgement of an absence at the core of what metaphysics sees as the self-evidence of the self-existent, then an ultimate space is at last created for an instantiation of the "eternal".

But this prefiguration of the eternal is not identical with the metaphysical concept of "eternity." The notion of eternity is merely the metaphysical underside to the equally tendentious notion of time as substance. What deconstruction prefigures is the prospect of *parousia*, that is, "final presence", which can only be prefigured because it is somehow veiled within the darkness of the unsaid, the inescapable alterity of every representation and predication. When theological thinking thinks *parousia* in this context, it thinks the end of theology, for theology is, conventionally speaking, the apologetics of the old eon.

At the same time, we must not let the thought of *parousia*, which arises from the theological thought of the "difference" between final presence and the Scholastic representation of God as Being itself, between the so-called "last things" of a highly symbolized eschatology and the "first principles" of metaphysical reasoning, become just another ragged and obscure tessera within the qualified language of "deconstructionism" per se. We learn elsewhere into what desert we have trekked when we take account of the fundamental problems of interpretation which have apparently bewitched both physics and psychology, which in the modern era have presumed to have uncovered the macrodeterminants of the external and internal worlds respectively. For physics, the elusive riddle of time, institutionalized by the still unresolved debate between Einstein and quantum theorists over whether both past and future events can be "geometrically" located somewhere within a gridlike, four-dimensional continuum or whether they depend on the conscious intervention of the observer, has not been satisfactorily answered.[24] A possible settlement of this dilemma surprisingly may require a renewed appreciation of Kant, whose "transcendental" critique is compared by one writer to a beacon in a lighthouse, confirming for the scientific investigator that one is "in sight of land."[25] Kant's understanding of time as the condition of unity of conscious representations anticipates the latest formulation of theoretical physics, which supersedes in many respects both the Einsteinian and the earlier quantum interpretations, that the "temporal" may not refer to a separate dimension at all, but to the co-

---

[24] For the relatively recent scientific and related philosophical debates in this area, see among others T. Gold (ed.), *The Nature of Time* (Ithaca, NY: Cornell University Press, 1967); J. R. Lucas, *Space, Time, and Causality* (Oxford: Oxford University Press, 1984); Henry Mehlberg, *Time, Causality, and the Quantum Theory: Studies in the Philosophy of Science* (Dordrecht: D. Reidel, 1980); Jiri Zeman (ed.), *Time in Science and Philosophy* (Amsterdam: Elsevier, 1971); David R. Griffin, *Physics and the Ultimate Significance of Time* (Albany, NY: State University of New York Press, 1986).

[25] David Park, *The Image of Eternity: Roots of Times in the Physical World* (Amherst, MA: University of Massachusetts Press, 1980), p. 111.

ordinating principle of rotating and reciprocally interwoven facets of an infinite "superspace", manifesting from moment to moment as the variable order of things.

Here physics and psychology converge, especially if the former stands for the search for "unified field" within the expanse of visible creation and the latter is by whatever view analogous to Augustine's delving for his Maker within the shoreless ocean of personal memory. Memory is not only the recovery of the unsaid, it is the redemption of time, as Lacanian psychoanalysis shows us through a glass darkly. Psychology, for Lacan, is ultimately a slow dredging up of *la parole qui dure*, the primal *logos* which is encrypted in the unconscious, including its delusions and fantasies. The unconscious is language, because language is time, and time is what holds the "repressed" and the transient presentation of speech together in a unity of significance. Time, Lacan tells us, joins together "the Symbolic and the Real." Time "presents itself first of all in the total duration of the analysis, and implies the sense to be given to the termination of the analysis, which is the question which must precede that of the signs of its end."[26] The ending of analysis in the proximate sense is the bringing to light out of the darkness what "time has forgotten." Time itself, however, can never be fully remembered, because time is what makes memory possible. It is what makes the thought of the divine, and therefore theological thinking, possible as well.

The thinking into time, and *through time,* of theological thinking is required now of all who profess to be theologically, or philosophically, disposed. The deconstruction of the "text" of God, which is all that has been said so far of God, allows the temporality behind what we mean when we talk about God come into full play. In fine, we are calling for a reformation of theology that never took place with the reformation of the church. If we may borrow Luther's famous shibboleth, we must *let God be God.* But we must never let God become the "final word." As Herder once asked: "What proof is there of the existence of a single word which only God could invent?"[27] The answer is none. Neither is there any proof of the invention of the single word "God." That is why we must in our theological wanderings navigate "by faith alone". Yet faith is not a solitary walk among the crumbling monuments of the ancients. It is, in truth, an *eschatological overture.*

---

[26] Jacques Lacan, *The Language of the Self,* trans. Anthony Wilden (Baltimore: The Johns Hopkins Press, 1968), p. 74.

[27] Johann G. Herder, *On the Origin of Language,* trans. John H. Moran and Alexander Gode (New York: Frederick Ungar, 1966), p. 158.

INDEX

Abrams, M. H., 8n, 96n
Agrippa, Cornelius, 38
Altizer, Thomas J. J., 12n, 85–7, 108, 117n
Anaximander, 44
Antichrist, 85
Aquinas, Saint Thomas, 6, 9, 29, 47
Aristotle, 30, 37, 44, 74–75, 80, 99, 108, 117–21, 140–2, 144–5, 148
Aristotelian logic, 121–2, 143n
Arnheim, Rudolf, 53
Arnold, Matthew, 96
Augustine, Saint, 34, 49, 101–2, 116, 145–6, 153
Aune, Bruce, 16n
Ayer, A. J., 118

Bacon, Francis, 29, 37–8, 93n; Baconianism, 30n
Baly, Dennis, 146
Barth, Karl, 11, 14–15, 18, 23, 105–6, 133, 138
Barthes, Roland, 150
Bell's theorem, 55, 70n, 72, 74–5
Berkeley, Bishop, 76
Bertallanfy, Ludwig, 84
Bohm, David, 41, 57–9, 63, 70, 74–6, 85
Bohr, Niels, 43, 56, 63, 72
Boltzmann, Ludwig, 81
Born, Max, 57
Broglie, Louis, 57
Bronowski, Jacob, 48
Brumbaugh, Robert, 144n
Buddhism, 122
Bultmann, Rudolf, 6, 9, 13, 17, 132, 136
Burtt, E. A., 22

Calvin, John, 25
Calvinism, 20, 31; neo-Calvinism, 34, 93
Campbell, Jeremy, 82
Capra, Fritjof, 20n, 72, 84–5

Cartesianism, see DESCARTES
"Cat paradox", 60–1
Chicago school, 117
Chisholm, Roderick, 16n
Christ, 15, 85, 127, 130
Churchill, James, 145n
Clement of Alexander, 40
Clift, Wallace, 14n
Cobb, John, 122
Cochrane, Lydia, 143n
Coleridge, Samuel Taylor, 95
Computers, 30, 52, 66
Complementarity, 72
Comte, Auguste, 137
Condillac, Etienne Bonnot, 111
Conjugate variables, 45–7, 51, 62
Copenhagen interpretation, 43, 56
Copernicus, 79
"Cosmic supervisor", 64–6
Crossan, John Dominic, 25

Dante, 39
Darwin, Charles, 79
Davies, Paul, 20n
Death of God, 24, 85–7, 98–9, 108
Deconstruction, 18, 100, 105–24, 132, 135, 138, 141–2, 146, 151–2; as "double science", 129; *Deconstruction and Theology*, 25n, 105n, 117n
Dee, John, 38
de Man, Paul, 99, 117
Demonstratio, 121; *demonstratio Christiana*, 13
Derrida, Jacques, 105–10, 115, 117, 122–4, 129–30, 132–4, 136–7, 149–50
Descartes, Rene, 29, 31, 33, 37, 42, 47, 55, 97, 113–480; neo-Cartesianism, 66
d'Espagnat, Bernard, 61–2, 77
Dewitt, Bryce, 61n, 66
Difference, 109, 115, 123, 132–4; theological thought of difference, 151

DATE DUE

NOV 12 1988			

HIGHSMITH 45-102   PRINTED IN U.S.A.